Painting Your Home: Exterior

Julian Cassell & Peter Parham

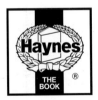

Haynes
THE BOOK
®

Contents

Introduction

Painting the exterior of your home is a large and demanding task. As well as decorating the house, you are also protecting and preserving it from aspects of the weather – including strong sunlight, rain and fluctuations in temperature. Keeping exterior walls, wood and metalwork in a sound condition is a necessity to avoid damage that may affect the interior.

It can be difficult to choose colours and finishes – especially with the large variety available today – so 'Ideas and Choices' will help you to make vital decisions.

With such a large-scale project, it is important to plan the work carefully. 'Planning and Preparation' goes into considerable detail on sound preparation and the benefits it produces.

Every technique that you may require is tackled in 'Painting' with additional ideas on economic and efficient ways of applying exterior coverings to produce the highest quality finish possible.

Finally 'Natural Wood Finishes' deals with stains, varnishes, oils and preservatives emphasising the general ease of use of these products which are continually improving year by year.

So, here is all you need to know to produce a long-lasting finish that may be enjoyed for many years to come. We wish you good fortune with the tasks ahead, and are certain that this book will be invaluable in completing the work successfully.

Ideas and Choices

Choosing colours and finishes runs very much in accordance with personal taste. However, there are issues of practicality and indeed occasional restrictions which must be considered.

Maintaining the character of your home may be important, so be sure to consider the architecture, and period influences if applicable. Further research into original finishes and colour schemes can often be rewarding. However, do bear in mind that your house may be in a conservation area and therefore there may be subjects to limits on colour choice.

Such constraints aside, try to seek inspiration from other houses or photographs you have admired, coupled with the necessary practical issues and information contained within this chapter.

This chapter contains

Painting masonry

Clearly, walls are the largest surfaces on a house and are therefore the most dominant aspect in the overall appearance of your home. When it comes to choosing colours or finishes there are general guidelines that may be observed. Pale colours appear to expand surface areas whereas darker colours tend to contract them. Darker colours do not show the dirt readily but lighter colours tend to produce a more reflective, brighter appearance.

Before making final decisions and purchasing the full quantity of paint, try some test areas. Experiment both in sunlight and shade. Be sure to consider what other colours or finishes are being used on windows and doors, and whether the selections will complement each other.

◀ Smooth render, painted white, is a safe but extremely practical use of colour for highlighting other features and providing a perfect backdrop for plants and garden accessories. Selective use in a courtyard or patio area, for example, will immediately brighten up dark, dingy corners giving a light, airy feel and impression of space.

► Textured coatings or paint are practical, hard-wearing finishes. They also add depth to wall surfaces and contrast well with other masonry surfaces.

▼ When choosing colours it is often necessary to try and complement other aspects of the property, such as the garden, architectural features that need highlighting, or in this case, blending the smooth render colour with natural stone.

▲ The use of colour on masonry also helps to match up two different surfaces. Some houses often look slightly disjointed if they combine too many types of masonry. Therefore blending the two together can help form a more complete and harmonious effect.

Painting wood and metal

All the miscellaneous features present on exteriors – such as doors, window frames, gutters, downpipes, fascia boards – require some sort of decoration. Depending on how attractive they are, they may be either highlighted, to accentuate a characteristic, or blended in, to camouflage a less appealing item.

The examples below illustrate some of the possibilities, as well as dealing with the practical issues of all exterior decoration. For example, choosing a paint or natural wood finish which has a long life expectancy must be balanced against its decorative qualities. There is a great deal of choice available, so think carefully about how these details may transform and personalise the look of your home.

◀▼ If you are lucky enough to have hardwood windows or doors, they will stand out from any other feature on the house. Apart from the fact that they will outlast the lifespan of softwood, their appearance, if looked after, will improve with age. Therefore choose treatments that have a transparent finish to enable the natural beauty of the wood to show through.

◀▼ On properties which have little or no painted masonry, using bold colours on woodwork can add to the general appearance of a house. Dark colours, as well as hiding dirt, add character and give a homely, 'lived-in' look. The high-gloss finish on both the front door (left) and garage door (below) is easy to keep clean and very durable, while still being highly decorative. The mid-sheen, opaque stain applied to the windows and frames complements the green, resulting in a simple yet effective co-ordination of colour.

▲ Purely practical items such as garden fences or picnic tables can be decorated to produce an attractive finished product. Timber preservatives now come in a range of colours as well as providing their usual protective qualities.

Paint finishes

Almost all paints suitable for the exterior of houses can be divided into two broad categories: water-based and solvent-based.

Water-based paints have increased in popularity over recent years, mainly because they are easy to use and are environmentally friendly. Solvent-based paints are more traditional. They are predominantly based on white spirit and are less user-friendly than their water-based counterparts.

	PRODUCT DESCRIPTION	SUITABLE SURFACES
PRIMER	Watery, dilute appearance specifically formulated to seal bare surfaces.	Use stabilising primer for masonry. All purpose primers are available
PRIMER-UNDERCOAT	A primer and undercoat in one, providing base for top coat(s).	Bare wood
UNDERCOAT	Dull, opaque finish providing ideal base for application of top coat(s).	Any primed surface.
SMOOTH MASONRY PAINT	Flat matt or mid sheen finishing paint. Majority are water based.	Most masonry surfaces.
TEXTURED MASONRY PAINT	Textured, 'gritty' matt or mid sheen finishing paint. Majority are water-based..	Most masonry surfaces.
TEXTURED FINISHING COATING	Highly textured, thick, paint coating	Most masonry surfaces
GLOSS	Polished, shiny finishing paint.	Any undercoated surface, ideally wood or metal.
METAL FINISHING PAINT	Mid sheen or gloss, available in a number of smooth or textured finishes.	Any bear or previously painted metal surfaces, excluding aluminium.
VARNISH	Translucent natural wood finish available in gloss, semi-gloss or matt, totally sealing surface.	All bare wood. May be applied over most previously stained surfaces.
STAIN	Deep penetrating natural wood finish. Variety of sheens available.	All bare wood. Darker colours may be applied over previously stained surfaces.
OIL	Penetrating natural wood treatment.	All bare wood, although hardwoods produce the best finishes.
TIMBER PRESERVATIVE	Highly penetrative wood preserver.	All bare or previously preserved wood.

Apart from these, there are some proprietary paints that need specific handling and application techniques. Remember to pay particular attention to the manufacturer's guidelines in such cases. The table below provides all the information you may need about the majority of paint and wood finishes, both water- and solvent-based.

Always read the manufacturer's guidelines for each product as there may be small variations in the categories outlined below.

MAIN QUALITIES	LIMITATIONS	APPLICATION METHOD
Excellent sealer enabling application of further coats of paint. Many have highly preservative formulation.	Only use is on bare or unstable surfaces.	Brush.
Easy to use, timesaving, quick drying.	Only available water-based.	Brush, roller, conventional or airless spray.
Hard wearing.	Lengthier application procedure compared to primer undercoat.	Brush or roller.
Hardwearing, most contain fungicide. Spreads further than textured counterparts.	Shows surface imperfections more clearly than textured equivalents.	Brush, roller conventional or airless spray
Hides surface imperfections, most contain fungicide.	Poor spreading capacity compared to smooth masonry paint.	Brush, roller or conventional spray.
Extremely hardwearing, flexible, hides cracks and surface imperfections.	Very low spreading capacity and therefore expensive to use.	Trowel/Float, roller, or conventional spray.
Very hardwearing decorative finish. Easy to clean.	Application takes longer than most other paints, and a sound technique is required to produce the desired finish.	Brush or roller.
Hardwearing, prevents rust.	Poor finish on large surface areas.	Brush, roller or aerosol.
Highly decorative and easy to clean, some contain fungicide.	Not very durable.	Brush.
Hardwearing. Enhances the grain and features of natural wood.	Difficult to strip or change colour once applied, so care is needed in initial choices.	Brush.
Can be used mainly as a nourishing preservative or provide a polished finish.	Regular applications required. Extra care required when disposing of cloths as some oils are highly combustible.	Brush and/or cloth. Cloth for removing surplus.
Easy to apply, very effective treatment against decay.	Regular applications needed to maintain colour	Brush, conventional or airless spray.

Order of work

It is vital to use the correct order of application for whatever finish you have chosen. The illustrations below show what products are required for each particular finish and the order in which they should be applied. Missing out a stage will not only affect the quality of the finish, but also reduce the protective capacity of your chosen system and therefore shorten the lifespan of decoration.

MASONRY PAINT ON NEW RENDER

1 Bare render
2 First coat of masonry paint
3 Second coat of masonry paint

MASONRY PAINT ON OLD RENDER

1 Old, painted masonry surface
2 Fungicide
3 Stabilising solution/primer
4 First coat of masonry paint
5 Second coat of masonry paint

WATER-BASED vs SOLVENT-BASED: THE PROS AND CONS

	WATER-BASED	SOLVENT-BASED	COMMENTS
EASE OF APPLICATION	• • • • •	• • •	Water-based tend to be much easier to apply, with less 'brushing out' required.
DRYING TIME	• • • • •	•	Much quicker turn-around between coats with water-based paints.
LOW ODOUR/TAINT	• • • • •	•	White-spirit smell of solvent-based paints can be overpowering. Minimal problem with water-based.
WASHABILITY	• • •	• • • • •	Surfaces painted with solvent-based paints are easiest to clean.
DURABILITY	• • •	• • • • •	Solvent-based are more hard-wearing, although water-based are catching up with improved formulation.
BRUSHMARKS	• •	• • • •	More evident in water-based, although improving all the time.
COLOUR RETENTION	• • • •	• • •	White solvent-based (especially) tends to yellow with age.
CLEANING TOOLS	• • • • •	•	Water-based easily cleaned with water and mild detergent. Solvent-based is a lengthier process requiring white spirit.
USER-FRIENDLY	• • • •	•	All health and safety guidelines make water-based products a better option than their solvent-based counterparts.

OIL-BASED PAINT ON BARE WOOD

1 Bare Wood
2 Knotter on bare wood knots
3 Primer (pink) or preservative primer (green)
4 Undercoat: two coats recommended
5 Gloss

WATER-BASED PAINT ON WOOD

1 Bare wood
2 Knotter on bare wood knots
3 Primer-undercoat
4 Gloss: two coats recommended

WOOD STAIN

1 Bare wood
2 Preservative base coat (solvent-based systems only)
3 First coat of stain
4 Second coat of stain. (Third coat may be required for water-based systems)

VARNISH

1 Bare wood
2 Preservative base coat
3 First coat of varnish
4 Second coat of varnish

WOOD OIL

1 Bare wood
2 First coat of oil
3 Second coat of oil

METAL FINISHING PAINT

1 Bare or previously painted metal
2 First coat proprietary metal-finishing paint
3 Second coat metal-finishing paint (if necessary)

Planning and Preparation

Exterior decorating projects are usually on a large scale, so by using the right materials and equipment and following a logical order of work, you will reduce both the time and effort needed to complete the job.

Thorough preparation not only makes painting easier, but ensures that the result looks good and protects your home for as long as possible.

Tools

When choosing and purchasing tools and equipment, always opt for quality rather than quantity. A few well-selected, superior items will be far more use than buying cheap kits which often contain many articles that you will never use.

It is not necessary to purchase the complete range of tools, as listed here. Instead, build up your equipment gradually. Also, if you have limited use for an item, especially the more expensive ones such as scaffold towers or sprayers, it may be more sensible to consider hiring, rather than an outright purchase.

Preparation

Slot-head screwdrivers

Cross-head screwdrivers

Chisels

Scraper
A broad, rigid blade for removing old paint finishes

Filling knife
A flexible blade helps to push filler into cracks and holes

Putty knife

Tape measure

Chalk line
Marks a long, straight line

Spirit level

Bucket

Sponge

Hammer

Pliers

Plier wrench
Similar to pliers, but has an adjustable, locking head to get a good grip

Dusting brush

Wire brush
Removes loose paint when repairing metal

Filler dispenser
A universal frame that can take a variety of filler and sealant tubes

Electric sander
For large areas

Electric hot-air gun
For stripping paint or varnish

Electric drill

Trowel

Float

Hawk

Access

Step-ladder

Ladder extension

Scaffold tower

Trestles and plank
Make a sturdy platform when working up high, or can support doors for painting

Protection

Protective gloves
Waterproof, to keep irritants off hands

Goggles
Keep dust, spray and chemicals out of eyes

Dust masks
(disposable)

Respirator mask
Protection against very fine dust and fumes

Dust sheet

Painting

Lid opener

Stirring stick

Paint kettle

Paintbrushes

Angle-headed paintbrush
Ideal for painting window bars and rebates

Varnish brushes

Brush comb

Cleaning system box

Roller cage and sleeves
Different sizes and textures of sleeve will fit on the same roller cage

Roller tray

Airless sprayer

Airless spray gun

Ladder safety

Painting the exterior of a house will almost inevitably involve work up a ladder, therefore it is important to know how to position a ladder correctly and to be aware of all the safety rules. Aluminium and other lightweight ladders are lighter, more durable and therefore easier to use than traditional wooden ladders. For all-purpose use the best buy is an extension ladder which consists of two ladders that can be used separately or joined together to gain access to high areas around the home.

TOOLS: Ladder, hammer, ladder stand-off, roofing attachment

MATERIALS: Pads of cloth, masking tape, wooden board, batten, rope, wooden stakes

POSITIONING A LADDER

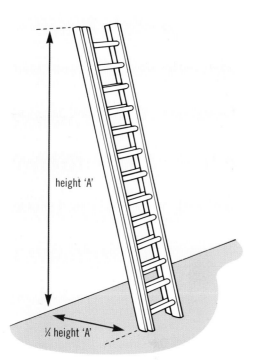

height 'A'

¼ height 'A'

To raise a ladder to an upright position, place it flat on the ground with the bottom feet of the ladder at the base of a wall. Go to the other end of the ladder, pick up the top rung and hold it above your head. Moving hand over hand gradually 'walk' the ladder up into a position where it is vertical against the wall. Now move the bottom feet out into a position where the distance from the base of the ladder to the bottom of the wall is one quarter of the distance from the bottom of the wall to the top of the ladder. At whatever height you use the ladder, always maintain this angle.

SAFETY CHECKLIST

1 Position the ladder correctly, taking extra care on uneven ground.
2 Never over-reach: get down and move the ladder to a new position.
3 Never go up a ladder higher than having the top rung waist height.
4 Never rest a ladder on guttering or downpipes.
5 Never leave a ladder unattended.
6 Always try to keep one hand on the ladder.
7 Regularly check the ladder – especially a wooden one – for any damage or wear.
8 Never rush when climbing up a ladder.

WALL PROTECTION

To protect wall surfaces from being scraped during painting, bind the top two stays of the ladder with pads of cloth held securely in place with masking tape.

SOFT GROUND

Most modern ladders have rubber feet which prevent any movement on hard surfaces. On uneven or soft ground, place the base of the ladder on a board. A batten, attached to the back of the board, will reduce the risk of movement.

EXTRA STABILITY

If the ground you are working on is soft and spongy, take the extra precaution of roping one of the bottom rungs of the ladder on to two stakes hammered securely into the ground.

USEFUL ATTACHMENTS

Ladder stand-off

This will make it considerably easier to work on protruding fascia or barge boards. Stand-offs are are clipped on to the top two to three rungs, thus bringing the top of the ladder away from the wall.

Roofing ladder attachments

These can be bolted on to most modern ladders. They enable you to reach dormer windows on a pitched roof. The roofing attachment hooks over the ridge of the roof so you are able to climb up the ladder with no fear of it slipping.

Scaffold towers

For the higher areas around your home, scaffold towers provide a more robust alternative to ladders. They are made out of strong lightweight alloy sections that clip together easily to make a stable working platform. This can be adjusted in height to whatever level is required. Scaffold towers are expensive to buy, however, so hiring is advisable.

Always check the general condition of a tower before using it. Older varieties have often been constructed from ferrous metals so beware of rusting joints or any distorted sections. Make sure that the standing platforms, or planks, are in sound condition.

TOOLS: Spirit level, rope, base plates for uneven ground

1 Although it is easier to build a scaffold tower if two people work together, it is perfectly possible to build it on your own. Always begin by attaching the wheels to the base sections. Make sure that the brake locks are working and apply them to all four wheels before continuing to add to the structure.

2 Once the bottom sections have been clipped together, use a spirit level to make sure that you are beginning the construction from a sound, level base. Most tower wheels can be adjusted to help with alignment. On soft ground or turf, place the wheels on a solid board or plank to provide stability.

3 Stabilisers should always be attached to at least the two corners of the tower that are furthest from the wall. This prevents the possibility of the tower toppling back away from the wall. If you do not have proper scaffold stabilisers, use roped-on ladders to brace the tower in a similar fashion.

A TYPICAL DESIGN FOR A SCAFFOLD TOWER

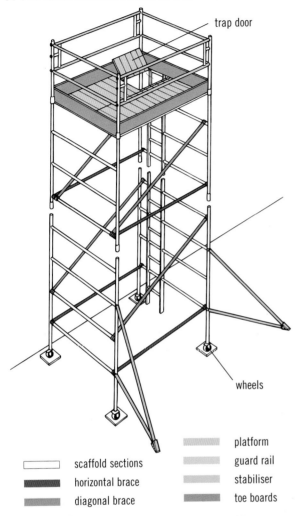

trap door

wheels

	platform
scaffold sections	guard rail
horizontal brace	stabiliser
diagonal brace	toe boards

4 Add further sections to the tower, depending on your needs. Always remember to attach a guard or safety rails on the top level.

5 Never climb up the outside of the tower as it may over-balance. Many towers have ladders built into the actual scaffold sections and a trap door platform to be used on the top level. However, should you be using a less elaborately designed tower, still remember to use the inside as the route for climbing and descending.

SCAFFOLD SAFETY

- Never join two scaffold towers together to gain extra height as each design of tower has a maximum level for stability.
- Only move the tower while it is fully erected if you are on solid level ground, as once the stabilisers have been removed, the whole structure becomes very top heavy.
- Don't leave any tools on the tower while moving it as they may fall, causing injury.

Clearing the way

Before any work can begin it is essential to remove any obstacles that restrict access to outside walls. Plants and shrubs need consideration as there is nothing more irritating than trying to hold a stray branch away from an area you are painting, and in fact this would be dangerous to attempt while up a ladder.

TOOLS: Ladder, secateurs, dust sheet, spade, screwdriver, bucket, plier wrench

1 Use a pair of secateurs or garden shears to trim back creepers and shrubs. This is especially important around guttering as overgrown vegetation will quickly block gutters, causing joints to leak. Such leaks will cause water damage to decorating which has been carried out on the walls, or even windows, below.

2 If possible, remove guttering to allow easy access to fascia boards. Plastic guttering will normally unclip easily; a slot-headed screwdriver is often useful to gently lever the clips holding up the guttering. Other guttering, such as metal, is often more difficult to take down and may need to be painted in position (see pages 66–67).

ELECTRICAL SAFETY

The mains electricity supply enters many houses through cables located at a high level. Extra caution needs to be taken when working close to such a hazard, especially when a ladder is being used. Contact your local electricity board to find out its recommended safety procedure and whether it needs to bind the cables with non-conductive sleeves before starting any repair or painting work to avoid any risk of electric shock.

3 Shrubs and plants on trellises up against walls are common obstacles. Wherever possible, unfasten any supporting wires or screws and gently pull the trellis or shrub forward, away from the wall, on to a dust sheet.

4 To reduce the risk of damaging a plant, use a bucket to support its weight. Make sure that everything is covered with a dust sheet, as this prevents any contamination by overspray when you start to paint.

5 Where there is no clear dividing line between the wall and the level of the ground, use a spade to pull back 5–10cm (2–4in) of soil or gravel away from the base of the wall. By doing this you will avoid getting dirt or grit in the paintbrush when painting at this low level and it will ensure a neat finish at ground level when the soil is replaced, after painting has been completed.

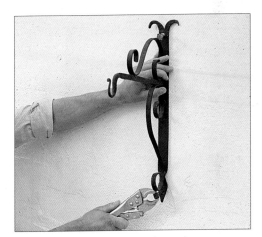

6 Removable metalwork, such as hanging basket brackets or light fittings, should also be taken down at this stage. This speeds up the painting process by giving an obstacle-free wall and also allows you to paint such items with greater ease (see pages 76–77).

Types of masonry

When planning to paint a bare masonry wall, you need to consider whether it is, in fact, suitable for a painted finish. Some surfaces accept paint better than others, and some types of masonry finish would be completely spoiled by the application of paint.

Outlined below are some of the more common types of masonry that you may have on your house.

RENDER	TEXTURED FINISHES	TYROLEAN

New render should be allowed to dry out thoroughly before it is painted. It then provides a perfect surface for painting. Rendered finishes vary a great deal, ranging from very smooth to rough cast.

Most textured finishes are self coloured and have been applied by a trowel and/or a roller. However, they may be over-painted successfully once they are discoloured or shabby from general wear and tear.

This is a different type of textured finish that is splattered on to the wall using a special hand-held machine. It is self coloured but, like other textured finishes, can be successfully overpainted if desired.

BRICKS

Common house bricks may be painted, but poor paint adhesion can sometimes be a problem. Bricks that have been given a glazed finish should not be painted over especially.

BREEZE BLOCKS

Normally used for internal wall blockwork, but are often found used for small exterior retaining walls. Paint application is difficult because they have a porous surface that is full of tiny holes.

NATURAL STONE

There are many different types of stone, but they are not normally painted, as they have a natural beauty already. Also, painting can be difficult because the surface starts to flake and crumble.

RECONSTRUCTED STONE

Many different varieties, all of which are made from crushed stone moulded into easy-to-use building blocks. Their natural attractiveness reduces the need for painting, but they will accept paint if required.

Identifying masonry problems

Exterior wall surfaces are constantly under attack from the elements. As well as temperature changes and the destructive properties of water in its various forms, general wear and tear and poor decoration in the past all contribute to the breakdown of a masonry surface.

It is important to recognise and remedy any problems before you begin to decorate. The most common are outlined below.

EFFLORESCENCE

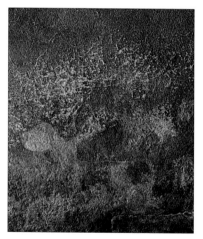

Caused by mineral salts within the masonry reacting with water and crystallising on the surface. Scrape away deposits and do not paint the wall until it has dried out thoroughly. When painting over an area that has had efflorescence, only use water-based paints as they will allow any remnants of moisture to dry through the painted surface.

BLOWN RENDER

The render layer on a wall may sometimes break away from its block base, making the wall surface very unstable. This is mainly caused by expansion and contraction of water trapped underneath (see Blown Bricks). Render tends to blow in localised areas and should therefore be removed and patch filled (see pages 36–37).

RUST STAINS

Caused by external metal fittings that have corroded and washed down the wall in the rain, causing an unsightly stain. May also be caused by old rusting nails or metal fragments below the paint surface that have bled through. To remedy, ferrous metal fittings should be painted and stains cleaned down and sealed with an oil-based undercoat.

BLOWN BRICKS

Caused by water, trapped below the brick surface, expanding and contracting with extreme changes in temperature, very gradually breaking down the brick. Remove flaky debris and stabilise before painting (see pages 34–35).

MOULD/ALGAE GROWTH

Often found in the small damp areas around leaking gutters or downpipes. Once established, mould growth can become very extensive and must be treated thoroughly before painting (see pages 34–35).

CRACKS

Caused by slight movement in the building. If extensive, cracking should be examined by a professional to check for major subsidence, smaller cracks can simply be filled with cement or exterior filler (see pages 36–37).

FLAKING PAINT

Caused by poor preparation when previously decorated or by water penetration. Must be scraped back to a sound surface before repainting (see pages 34–35).

MORTAR DECAY

Damp and extreme temperature changes gradually break down the cement between blocks or bricks. Repoint before painting or damp proofing (see pages 74–75).

LICHEN

Like algae, lichen tends to take hold initially in a small area but spreads rapidly. Scrape away all signs of growth and treat the area with fungicide (see pages 34–35).

Identifying wood problems

Wood is even more susceptible than masonry to problems caused by direct sunlight, and to the devastating decay caused by water. For example, a window situated in direct sunlight for the majority of the day is more prone to cracking joints than a window in a dark damp corner which will be more at risk to rot and insect infestation.

Regular painting, using the correct systems, will prevent these problems occurring and therefore will reduce the risk and the expense of having to replace doors and windows.

DETERIORATING PUTTY

Cracking or loose putty is usually caused by water seeping into a gap behind it, caused by slight expansion and contraction of the glass. This, linked with direct sunlight, can gradually break down the main body of the putty and risk deeper water penetration into the wood. Depending on the severity, re-putty or fill and make good (see pages 44–45).

BLEEDING KNOTS

Caused by failure to seal bare knots in the wood before it was primed. Sometimes, even if knots have been sealed, intense sunlight will still cause them to bleed further. To remedy, scrape away excess sap and seal with knotting solution, or use a heat gun to remove any sap remaining in the knot before painting the surface (see pages 80–81).

FLAKING PAINT

Normally caused by ageing and the constant attack of the sun and rain. Alternatively, paint may have been applied over a surface that was ingrained with dirt or grease. Remove all the flaky material, with a scraper if necessary, sand the surface and clean it down thoroughly before re-priming and painting it again (see pages 40–41).

DENATURED WOOD

Strong sunlight will often bleach or discolour bare or preserved wood. If the wood is to have a natural wood finish, using a wood reviver will help to rejuvenate its colour before a new finish is applied (see pages 80–81).

CRACKED JOINTS AND PANELS

Expansion and contraction in wooden joints produces cracks that will be susceptible to water penetration. Rake out the cracks, prime and fill with a flexible filler that will accommodate further movement (see pages 42–43).

MOULD/ALGAE

Mould suggests the likelihood of a damp problem which must be cured and removed before any painting can take place. Wash down with fungicide and rinse thoroughly.

ROTTEN WOOD

Wood is rotted by water, and by wood-eating pests. In extensive cases, entire sections may need to be replaced. In small, localised areas, cut away loose material, treat and fill (see pages 40–41).

Paint and materials

It is always better to buy good-quality materials, as cheaper ones will not offer as much protection. Furthermore, having to add an extra coat of paint because you have chosen a low-cost, poor-covering alternative can lead to greater expense than if good paint had been purchased at first.

Here are most of the materials needed to carry out nearly all exterior painting work. As with tool purchase, be selective. For quantities of paint, check with both the table opposite and the product information on the back of the can.

BASIC SUPPLIES

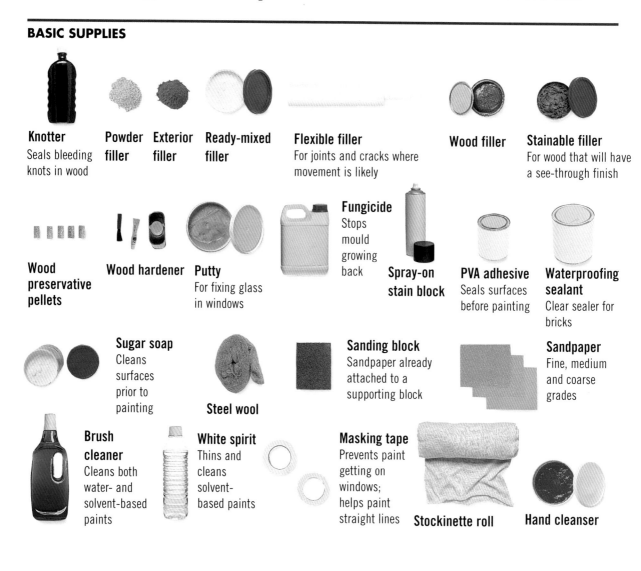

Knotter
Seals bleeding knots in wood

Powder filler

Exterior filler

Ready-mixed filler

Flexible filler
For joints and cracks where movement is likely

Wood filler

Stainable filler
For wood that will have a see-through finish

Wood preservative pellets

Wood hardener

Putty
For fixing glass in windows

Fungicide
Stops mould growing back

Spray-on stain block

PVA adhesive
Seals surfaces before painting

Waterproofing sealant
Clear sealer for bricks

Sugar soap
Cleans surfaces prior to painting

Steel wool

Sanding block
Sandpaper already attached to a supporting block

Sandpaper
Fine, medium and coarse grades

Brush cleaner
Cleans both water- and solvent-based paints

White spirit
Thins and cleans solvent-based paints

Masking tape
Prevents paint getting on windows; helps paint straight lines

Stockinette roll

Hand cleanser

Finishing

Primer, Undercoat

Paint, Stain, Varnish, Oil, Wood dye, Preservative

CAUTION

Some materials contain hazardous chemicals. Always remember to read the manufacturers' guidelines before handling them.

COVERAGE

Try to be as accurate as possible when measuring the surface area of walls and treat each wall or aspect of a house separately. The width of a wall may be easily measured by simply running a tape measure along its base. To measure height on a two-storey building, pick a point by eye which is about half the total wall height, measure to this level and simply double it to gain the total height.

Use common sense when making deductions in surface area for windows and doors. Clearly there is no need to worry about making allowances for doors, but the dimensions of large picture windows should be deducted from the overall area.

Gaining accurate surface areas for windows can be more difficult. With casement windows composed of many small panes and rails, use the dimensions of the window to obtain a basic surface area. For windows that consist of a pane of glass and little more, make deductions for the glass.

Paint coverages are greatly affected by surface porosity. Obviously, unpainted render will require much more paint than a wall that was previously painted, and so before making a large purchase buy a small quantity of paint and test to see how far it will spread. The table above right is only an approximate guide for surfaces of average porosity.

ACRYLIC/WATER-BASED

	sq m/litre	sq yd/gallon
Gloss	15	82
Primer/undercoat	10	55
Masonry paint (smooth surface)	12	65
Masonry paint (rough surface)	4	22
Wood stain	20	110

SOLVENT/OIL-BASED

Gloss	17	92
Primer	20	110
Undercoat	15	82
Oil	12	65
Timber preservative	10	55
Varnish	16	87
Wood stain	22	120

MICROPOROUS PAINTS AND FINISHES

Many products have what are referred to as microporous properties. This means that they allow moisture to dry out through the finished surface, but do not allow moisture to penetrate back inwards.

These are clearly excellent preservative qualities and therefore such products are ideal for exterior decoration.

However, if you are using these products to recoat over a finish which does not have the same properties rather than applying them directly on to untreated surfaces, the microporous effect of the new paint is considerably diminished.

Masonry preparation

Because the walls are the largest surface area on the exterior of a house, they require the most paint and therefore incur the greatest expense. Most masonry paints have a guaranteed life expectancy of up to ten years, but without sound preparation their life can be at least halved. Good preparation is therefore vital, and the amount of work required depends largely on whether the walls have been previously painted.

TOOLS: Scraper, 100–150mm (4–6in) brush, goggles, gloves, stiff brush, pressure washer, dust sheets

MATERIALS: Fungicide, stabilising solution

1 On old or previously painted walls, use a scraper to get rid of any flaky paint or loose material. Anything growing on the walls, such as lichen, must be completely removed.

2 Check for any signs of mould or algae growth. This is most likely to be present on older, previously painted render, but may also be found on newer unpainted surfaces. Apply fungicide liberally to all affected areas with a large 100–150mm (4–6in) brush; check the manufacturer's instructions as it may require dilution before application. Wear safety goggles and gloves as the fungicide is toxic.

3 On exterior walls that have a thick, extensive growth of either mould or algae it may be necessary to use a stiffer brush in order to remove the deposits completely. Scrub the affected area very thoroughly. In such cases, more than one application of fungicide may be required to clear the surface.

4 Leave the wall for at least 24 hours to allow the fungicide enough time to kill off all traces of mould or algae. Then thoroughly wash down all areas with clean water. A pressure washer is ideal, as it both cleans off any traces of fungicide and dead algae as well as removing any loose material that may have been missed during step 1. When using a pressure washer always wear goggles for protection against flying debris.

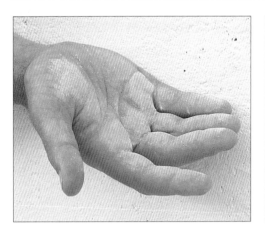

6 Such areas must be treated with a stabilising solution to bind the surface together so that it is able to accept paint. Wear protective goggles and gloves and apply to all affected areas making sure that they are

5 Once dry, check whether walls are sound and free from loose material of any nature. Some surfaces may still have a chalky or powdery texture from mortar/cement breakdown caused by general ageing.

completely covered. Using stabilising solution has the added advantage of reducing the porosity of the masonry. Paint will therefore go much further than on an untreated surface. Make sure that all areas are covered with dust sheets and windows and doors are protected or masked (see pages 50–51) as unwanted splashes are difficult to remove.

Filling masonry

Cracks and holes in masonry should be filled in, not only to make the finish as attractive as possible, but also because it is necessary in order to close off any routes where water might penetrate into the wall, and thereby into the house, forming damp patches and spoiling the interior decoration.

While modern masonry paint will cover up and seal hairline cracks, anything larger must be cleaned out and filled. Always use filler specifically designed for exterior use as all-purpose fillers are not sufficiently durable to withstand the harsh effects of weathering.

TOOLS: Dusting brush, filler board, filling knife, 50mm (2in) brush, sponge, bucket, hawk, plastering float

MATERIALS: Exterior filler, cement, sand, jug of water, mortar plasticiser/ household detergent, PVA adhesive

SMALL CRACKS

1 The crack must be freed of any loose debris such as small pieces of mortar, grit and cobwebs. If the material is very hard to shift, you may need to use a scraper, but most dirt can be cleaned out with a dusting brush.

2 Pour the required amount of exterior filler on to a filler board. Old paint-tub lids make excellent boards as they have a rim to prevent water pouring off, and as they are made of plastic they are easy to keep clean. Make a small depression in the centre of the filler with a filler knife and add water gradually, mixing into a wet, pliable consistency.

3 Use a small brush to wet the crack with water. This helps the filler to bond with the masonry and slows down the drying time, reducing the risk of shrinkage or cracking.

4 Use a filling knife to firmly press the filler into the crack, smoothing the surface as you go. Try to remove any excess filler from around the crack while the filler is still wet.

5 Wipe over the filler with a damp sponge. This reduces the need for sanding once it is dry which is difficult as exterior filler is coarser and harder than interior or all-purpose filler

LARGE HOLES

1 For larger holes, or areas of blown render, a sand-cement mix should be used for patching. Initially, mix dry in a ratio of 5 parts sand to 1 part cement. Add water gradually and mix to a wet, stodgy consistency. Add mortar plasticiser or a little household detergent to improve the workability of the mix.

2 Remove any loose debris from the hole and wet the area as covered in steps 1 and 3 above. A small quantity of PVA adhesive mixed with the water (1 part PVA : 5 parts water) will aid the bonding process between the mix and the wall surface. Transfer the cement mix to a hawk and use a plastering float to press the mix into the hole. This is often a messy process, so by holding the hawk below the area being filled, it is possible to catch the excess.

3 Smooth the surface of the wet render, matching it with the surrounding area. Allow it to dry slightly, then use a wetted float to polish the surface. You may need to repeat this if necessary. If the patch starts to bulge, this usually means the hole is too deep to fill in one go. Take back the patch to below the wall level, allow to dry and apply a second layer of the render mix.

Stripping wood

Modern paints have dramatically reduced the need to strip woodwork before they are reapplied. However, there are some instances when stripping is still necessary. For example, on surfaces covered by many layers of paint it is difficult to obtain an acceptable finish unless all the coats are stripped back to the bare wood; and if a transparent wood finish is to be used, such as stain or varnish, all traces of paint must be first removed.

There are two methods for paint removal: chemical stripping and using a hot-air gun.

TOOLS: Hot-air gun, trestles, scraper, shavehook, heat shield, old paintbrush, gloves, electric sander

MATERIALS: Chemical stripper, white vinegar, sandpaper, lint-free cloth, white spirit, steel wool

HOT-AIR GUN

1 If possible, remove the object to be stripped from its usual position. For example, lie a door flat on trestles to give easy access to all areas. Hold the nozzle of the hot-air gun approximately 5cm (2in) away from the painted surface. Leave it on one area long enough to allow the paint to melt and bubble, and scrape off the debris using a scraper or shavehook. Take care not to hold the nozzle of the gun in one place for too long as you risk setting light to the paint or scorching the wood.

2 When stripping areas that are close to glass, such as a window frame, most hot-air guns have heat shields which may be attached to the nozzle in order to protect the glass from cracking.

IDEAL TOOL

A shavehook is useful for stripping as its pointed corners can be used to remove paint from the most intricate areas, such as the corners of window frames.

CHEMICAL STRIPPING

1 Chemical strippers are available in liquid, gel, or paste forms so it is important to read the manufacturer's guidelines before use. The more liquid varieties should be applied in a dabbing motion using an old paintbrush. Do not brush out the stripper as it needs to be concentrated and densely applied in order to properly react with the paint. Wear protective gloves and apply paint strippers with care as they irritate the skin.

2 Leave the area for between ten minutes and half an hour to allow the stripper to break down the paint. Scrape away the bubbling debris using a shavehook. If all the paint does not come away at one time, further applications of stripper may be needed.

3 Once a surface is totally stripped, wash away any chemical remnants with clean water, or depending on the type of stripper used, clean down with white vinegar to neutralise the chemicals. Allow to dry and sand the wood thoroughly to produce a smooth, clean surface. An electric sander is ideal for large flat surfaces; always sand with the grain of the wood.

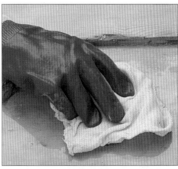

4 Finally, remove any dust from the surface by wiping down with a lint-free cloth dampened with some white spirit.

REMOVING INGRAINED PAINT

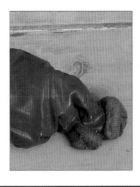

Paint that is lodged in the grain of wood can be removed by applying a small amount of chemical stripper to the area and rubbing the traces of paint away with some steel wool.

Woodwork preparation

By nature, wood is less hardwearing or durable than masonry and therefore requires more frequent attention. Even the highest quality paints will rarely last longer than five years on wood, making sound preparation essential.

General wear and tear, wet and dry rot, the onslaught of direct sunlight and temperature changes all contribute to surface breakdown and the need to redecorate. All the problems caused by weathering must be dealt with before painting can begin.

TOOLS: Bucket, sponge, scraper, dusting brush, electric drill, 15mm (½in) paintbrush, gloves

MATERIALS: Sugar soap or household detergent, wood hardener, preservative pellets, filler, sandpaper, primer

ALL SURFACES

Mix up a solution of sugar soap or ordinary household detergent and thoroughly wash down all the surfaces, whether they are damaged or not, to remove traces of dirt, grease and grime. When they are quite clean, rinse them down with clean water.

ROTTEN WOOD

1 Where the wood has rotted in small, localised areas it must be removed and the area filled. With a scraper, cut loose or decaying wood back to sound dry timber. When all the rot has been removed, dust away loose debris.

2 Apply some wood hardener to the bare wood. This is usually made up by mixing a hardening compound with another chemical solution, so follow the manufacturer's guidelines carefully. Saturate the affected area with the hardener.

3 As a further precaution to prevent rot from spreading, preservative pellets may be used. Drill a series of holes around the rotten area about 75mm (3in) apart. In the example shown here, it would be wise to progress along the entire length of the window sill.

4 Push a preservative pellet into each hole. They will slowly release a chemical that impregnates and therefore protects the wood from further rot. Make sure each pellet rests below the surface of the wood, then fill and seal the holes with the appropriate filler (see pages 42–43).

DAMAGED PAINTWORK

1 Less severely damaged areas must also be repaired. Where the old painted surface has blistered or flaked, use a scraper to remove all the unstable or loose material.

2 Sand the area of bare wood thoroughly, removing any loose pieces of paint or wood. Feather the edges of the sound paint in with the now bare area of wood.

3 Using a small brush – a 15mm (½in) brush is ideal for windows – prime the bare patch of timber, slightly overlapping the primer on to the surrounding painted wood.

Filling wood

Surfaces that have been filled and sanded smooth encourage water to run off. But as well as preventing water penetration, and therefore structural damage, filling all the holes and cracks in woodwork quite simply makes the finished result look better.

Although there is a variety of different wood fillers on the market, there are basically two categories: those mixed with water or hardeners and then sanded smooth when dry, and those which are flexible to cope with joint movement.

TOOLS: Filler board, filling knife, sanding block, shavehook, dusting brush, filler dispenser

MATERIALS: Powder filler, sandpaper, wood filler, small spatula, flexible filler, jug of water

POWDER FILLER

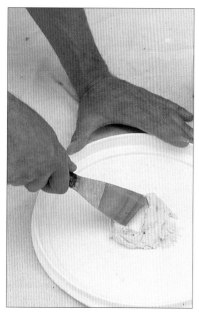  

1 All-purpose powder fillers are ideal for small nicks or holes on the surface of the wood. Pour the amount required on to a filler board and add water slowly, mixing with a filler knife into a smooth yet sturdy consistency.

2 Press the filler firmly into the hole leaving it slightly proud of the wooden surface. It may be necessary to move the filling knife across the surface of the filler two or three times to make sure that it is securely in place.

3 Allow the filler to dry and sand it back to a smooth finish, flush with the surrounding wood. For slightly deeper holes, it may be necessary to gradually build up layers of filler to obtain a perfectly smooth finish.

WOOD FILLER

1 For large holes or areas which have been treated for rot, a specialist wood filler is a sensible alternative. These fillers are usually supplied in the form of a thick paste which needs to be mixed with a hardening compound just before application. They tend to dry very quickly, so only mix up a small amount of filler at a time.

2 Manufacturers usually supply a small spatula for application. Work quickly, pressing the filler firmly into the hole. Again, fill the area slightly proud and sand it down when the filler has dried out. Further applications will normally be necessary to obtain a perfect finish, but the end result is extremely hard and durable.

FLEXIBLE FILLER

1 As its name suggests, flexible filler is ideal for cracked panels or any area where movement between different parts of the joint is likely. Use a shavehook to rake out loose material from cracked joints, then sand the area smooth. Clear away any debris with a dusting brush. It is vital to carry out any sanding at this stage as flexible filler cannot be sanded. Applying it should, therefore, be the last job before painting commences.

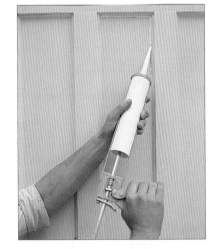

2 Carefully cut off the end of the nozzle of the tube and load it into the filler dispenser. Hold the nozzle next to the cracked joint and gradually move the nozzle down the crack, simultaneously pulling the trigger to form a bead of filler down the length of the crack.

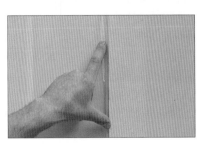

3 Run a wetted finger along the bead to form a smooth filled joint. This should withstand some flexing in the surrounding area.

Repairing puttywork

Putty is the protective barrier that not only holds glass in place in windows, but also prevents water seeping in under the glass and rotting the wood.

Putty is mainly damaged by direct sunlight cracking its surface so that water can seep behind it, lifting and loosening the bond between putty and wood. Two methods may be used to cure the problem: replacing seriously damaged sections, or simply filling minor cracking.

TOOLS: Scraper, dusting brush, 15mm (½in) paintbrush, putty knife, sanding block

MATERIALS: Primer, putty, powder filler, sandpaper

REPLACING PUTTY SECTIONS

2 Prime the exposed area of bare wood on the window, and allow to dry.

3 Knead a small amount of putty in your hands until it is pliable, then press it into the glass–wood junction.

1 Use a scraper to lift out any loose sections of putty. Dust out the area thoroughly to remove any dirt or debris.

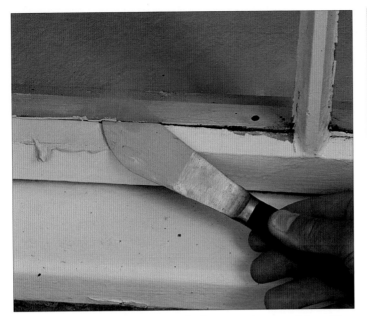

4 Use a putty knife to smooth the putty into position. To obtain a neat finish, keep the straight edge of the knife flush with the glass surface and the lower section resting on the wooden rail. This technique requires some practice so you may need to attempt it several times to produce the right result. Remove any excess putty and then allow the rest to dry completely, before priming the putty.

GLAZING-BEAD REPAIR

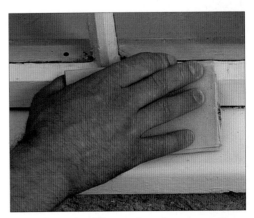

Panes of glass may also be held in place by solid wooden glazing beads. These are held in position by small pins or nails. To replace a damaged bead, use an old chisel or a screwdriver to prise the old bead loose. Before inserting a new bead, be sure to seal the glass–wood junction with a clear silicone sealant.

REPAIRING CRACKS

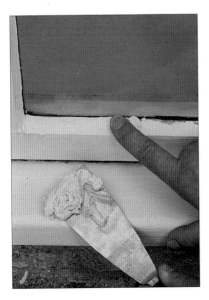

1 If the damaged area of putty is basically sound, and still firmly attached to the wood and glass, small cracks in the putty can be filled using an all-purpose powder filler. Remove any flaky paint from the putty, sand the surface and apply the filler with a finger, working it into every small crack.

2 Allow the filler to dry, then use a fine-grade sandpaper to smooth the suface, taking care not to scratch the edge of the glass with the sandpaper.

Removing broken glass

Panes of glass can crack because of frame expansion or contraction, but a more likely cause is an accidental knock, such as being hit by a stone or a ball.

There are obvious hazards when dealing with glass, but with care, removing a broken pane is a relatively simple operation. Keep pets and children away from the area while you are working and be sure to follow all the safety guidelines.

TOOLS: Gloves, goggles, hammer, old chisel, pliers, dusting brush, 15mm (½in) paintbrush

MATERIALS: Cardboard box, masking tape, sandpaper, primer

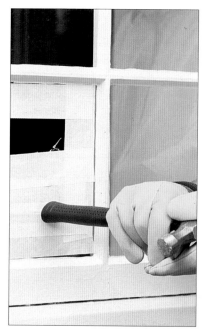

1 Any loose fragments of glass must be removed safely before repairs can be carried out. Wear thick protective gloves while handling the glass. Have a cardboard box at hand in which to put all the pieces so there is no danger of further injury.

2 Use masking tape to cover the glass that is still fixed in the window frame. This will help to prevent further fragmentation or shattering while the remaining broken pieces are removed. Apply strips of tape to all the areas of glass, sticking it on firmly.

3 Gently tap the remaining pane with the handle of a hammer. This should loosen the broken glass making removal much easier. Further shattering should not occur because of the masking tape, but goggles should be worn as a precaution.

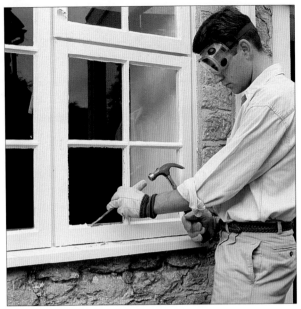

4 Once most of the broken glass has been removed, there may still be some pieces lodged around the edge of the frame, still held in by putty. Remove the glass and putty using a hammer and an old chisel to gradually tap away back to the solid wood rail. Again, goggles must be worn for safety.

WINDOW WITH GLAZING BEADS

In cases where the broken pane is retained with solid glazing beads, remove the beads initially using the same method as shown on page 45. Then continue with steps 2, 3, 6 and 7 below.

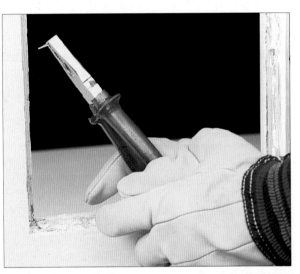

5 Use a pair of pliers to remove any retaining pins or nails from the wooden frame.

6 Sand the window rebate, then clear away any loose material with a dusting brush. Dispose of all the broken glass and debris safely, by sealing it in a sturdy cardboard box, for example.

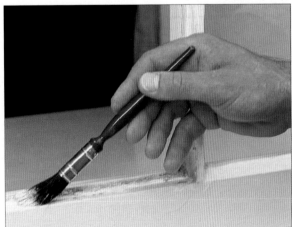

7 When the window is clear of all loose material, glass particles and dust, prime the bare wooden rebate with a small brush in preparation for a new pane of glass.

Inserting new glass

The most important factor when inserting a new window pane is buying the correct thickness of glass. Small windows should only require 3–4 mm (⅛in)-wide glass, whereas 5–6mm (¼in) is more suitable for larger windows or doors. If the broken pane was frosted or patterned, take a small sample of the broken glass to the supplier in order to find an exact match.

TOOLS: Tape measure, hammer, putty knife

MATERIALS: Glass, putty, dry powder filler, glazing pins, cardboard

1 Measure the exact width and height of the aperture, taking the measurement tight up to the rebate. Then deduct 3mm (⅛in) from each dimension to allow for the glass to be bedded into the putty, and to reduce any risk of future cracks caused by minor expansion or contraction of the glass. Be sure to measure from corner to corner on each side as the window may not be totally square.

2 Take a large quantity of putty and work it in your hands. This ensures that all the oil and any small lumps are mixed in well, producing a smooth pliable ball. It helps to cover your hands in a thin layer of dry powder filler before handling the putty, to soak up excess oil and make handling slightly easier.

3 Roll the putty into thin sausage-like lengths and firmly press them into and around the open window rebates.

4 Carefully place the new pane of glass into the aperture, allowing the edges of the glass to embed into the centre of the putty strips. Gently press the glass into place by applying pressure at all four corners and along the edge of the pane. Never apply any pressure to the centre of the pane as it might break.

5 Tap a glazing pin into the centre of each rebate. These hold the glass in while the putty dries and in later years if the putty decays. Do not put the pin directly against the glass as it may crack. Rest a piece of card against the glass to prevent scratches or another breakage. For a larger window use more glazing pins.

NEW PANES AND GLAZING BEADS

When replacing an old window pane on a window that uses glazing beads, measure for the glass as shown in step 1, but use a silicone sealant to bed the pane of glass into the window frame. The wooden beads, once secured back in place with glazing pins, will hold the glass in position.

6 Mould some more putty into sausage-like lengths. While they are still quite pliable, carefully press them into place over the edge of the glass and up to the rebate.

7 Use a putty knife to smooth the putty into place. The knife is designed to produce a straight precise line on the glass surface: see pages 44–45. Save excess putty to use in the future.

8 Trim excess putty from the inside of the glass using the sharp edge of the putty knife. Let the putty dry out for at least two weeks, depending on the weather, before priming and painting.

Masking up and covering

The sole purpose of masking up or covering an item is to prevent chemicals or paint from splashing on it. Apart from dust sheets protecting the ground, it is often necessary to mask certain areas or items on the wall. Small drops of paint accidentally spilt on a wooden window is not too much of a problem, but masking becomes more important with PVC windows that never require painting.

Although it is essential to mask carefully when spray painting, it is not always necessary to mask every area with such precision. For example, at ground level a temporary framework can be set up and moved between windows.

TOOLS: Bucket, sponge, hammer, plastic dust sheet, dust sheet

Materials: Sugar soap or household detergent, masking tape, nails, 2 lengths of wood, plastic bag

PRECISE MASKING

1 Before masking a PVC window, clean it down with a solution of sugar soap or household detergent. Although PVC does not decay or rot, it does need periodic cleaning. The clean surface will also help masking tape to stick and therefore make a tight seal.

2 Begin masking by running a band of tape around the edge of the window frame. Use a tape 20–25mm (¾–1in) wide as this will be thin enough to be flexible when moulding it around the contours of the window frame.

3 Use a plastic dust sheet to cover the window, attaching it to the masking tape with another, thicker 50mm (2in) tape to hold it securely in position. A clear plastic dust sheet allows light into the house which is preferable to being totally blacked out.

GENERAL COVERING

1 Measure the width of the largest ground-floor window and the greatest height to the top of a ground-floor window. Add 30cm (12in) to the height and cut two lengths of 50–60mm (2–3in)-square batten to the extra height, and to the width. Nail the lengths together in a T shape. Do not worry about precision, as it is only a rough frame.

2 Drape a dust sheet over the frame and lean it up against the wall so that the top of the T rests slightly above the window. It is now possible to roller or paint above the window without fear of any unwanted overspray. The frame may then be moved along to other windows to carry out the same function.

3 It is sometimes difficult to remove all accessories from walls before painting. Objects, such as electrical appliances, can be covered temporarily. Plastic bags are ideal. Make sure that the electrical supply is not turned on when the fitting is covered as this may cause a fire hazard.

SUCCESSFUL MASKING

Using tape to mask areas is a very helpful aid when trying to achieve a neat finish, but it is essential to remove the tape before the paint has hardened, otherwise you run the risk of tearing the paint and ruining the finish.

Painting

There is no doubt that this stage of decorating is the most rewarding. Suddenly, you begin to see the satisfying results of all your preparation. However, it is very important to use the correct techniques for adding paint as otherwise all your careful preparation will have been wasted. As well, keep to a logical order to avoid repeating any task unnecessarily and refer to Order of Work on pages 14–15 to check on the number coats a surface may require.

Only undertake painting when the weather is fine. Bad weather – even small sprinklings of rain – may not only reduce the paint's preservative qualities but also ruin the decorative finish. On the other hand, painting in direct sunlight speeds up drying times and makes the paint harder to spread. Ideally, choose a fine day and follow the shade.

This chapter contains

Preparation

As a general rule, start at the top of the house and work down. Fascias and guttering should be painted first, followed by the walls, followed by windows and doors. Leave any smaller accessories, such as outside lights or metal work, until last.

First, remove guttering for cleaning, or repaint it, before you clean or decorate the areas below. That way, if it rains during the decorating process, it does not matter if the lower areas get covered in water and debris from the roof, as they can be cleaned and prepared once the guttering is finished. Also, you avoid paint overspray spoiling the lower areas.

TOOLS: Dusting brush, lid opener, stirring stick, paint kettle, 2 buckets, dust sheet

MATERIALS: Paint, kitchen foil, stockinette or gauze cloth, large rubber band

PREPARING THE PAINT

1 Before opening the can, use a dusting brush to wipe the lid clean, as grit and dirt tend to collect around the rim. Otherwise, debris may fall into the paint when the lid is removed.

2 Prise the lid open with a blunt instrument. A tool designed for this task can be bought cheaply and saves damaging expensive items such as screwdrivers or chisels.

3 Some paints such as non-drip gloss must not be stirred before use, so always read the manufacturer's guidelines. Otherwise, most paints need a thorough stir. Use either a proprietary stirring stick or a piece of wooden dowel. As you stir, try to use a lifting motion. This brings up any sediment from the bottom of the can, and ensures that the pigments are mixed thoroughly into the rest of the paint.

4 It is advisable to decant the paint into a paint kettle for several reasons. First, the original can will stay cleaner for storage. Second, if any accident occurs, less paint is spilt. Third, it is clearly dangerous to carry a heavy can up a ladder which can easily throw you off balance, and finally if any debris gets into the kettle it can be cleaned out and refilled from the original can. Lining a paint kettle with tin foil will save time when cleaning it out or using a different colour.

5 When using paint left over from a previous job, you may find a skin has formed. Remove this from the can before attempting to stir. The paint may still have lumps so it is advisable to sieve it before use. Place some stockinette or gauze cloth over the kettle and hold it in place with a large rubber band. Pour the paint slowly into the kettle. This same method may be used to prevent insects and debris getting back into the main can when you replace the paint at the end of the day.

6 Some manufacturers will suggest that paint is thinned before application, usually on the first coat for porous masonry surfaces, or for practical reasons such as for applying paint with a sprayer (see pages 60–61). Make sure you use the correct thinner which is usually water for water-based paints or white spirit for solvent-based – but always read the manufacturer's instructions on the container. Use two calibrated buckets for this to be sure of accuracy with the thinning ratio. Stir the thinned paint thoroughly to ensure a consistent solution.

Using a roller

Covering large surfaces is quick and effective with a roller, so it is an ideal method for painting masonry. Rough or textured walls require a roller with a long pile to make sure that the paint gets into every indentation or hollow, so be sure to select the appropriate roller sleeve for the type of surface being painted before beginning work.

Always begin at the top and work down, and cover the ground with dust sheets as there will inevitably be a certain amount of unsightly overspray. Masking up round windows or doors may be necessary (see pages 50–51).

TOOLS: Roller sleeve, roller cage, roller tray, ladder roller tray, extension pole, battery operated roller, scissors, dust sheets

MATERIALS: Paint, clingfilm

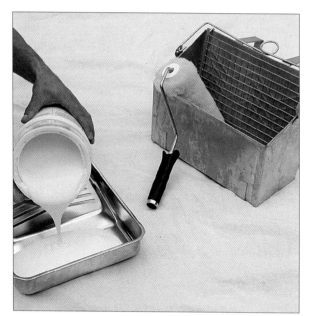

1 A roller tray consists of 2 parts: the paint reservoir, and a ribbed slope to wipe off excess paint and allow it to run back into the reservoir. Pour some paint into the reservoir, filling it to just below the start of the slope. If you are working up a ladder a tray specially designed to hook on to the ladder rungs must be used.

2 Dip the roller head into the paint and run it up and down the slope to distribute the paint evenly. Take care not to overload the roller head. Always try to keep the roller tray out of direct sunlight as glare off the paint will attract insects and the heat from the sun will quickly cause a skin to form on the surface.

TEMPORARY STORAGE

When temporary storage is needed – between coats, for example – cut off a short length of clingfilm and wrap it round the roller head, making sure to expel any trapped air. This saves having to wash out and dry the roller at regular intervals.

3 Move the loaded roller over the wall using even strokes. Each time the roller is reloaded, apply it to an unpainted surface and then work back to the previously painted area with overlapping strokes. On rough surfaces, you may have to apply a little more pressure to the roller on the wall to make sure the paint covers adequately.

IDEAL TOOLS

Extension pole
Attached to the roller handle, this is extremely effective for painting areas from ground level which you would normally be unable to reach. As well, an extension pole can reduce the amount of bending when reloading the roller or when painting the lower areas at ground level. However, roller extensions should not be used when painting up a ladder as you need two hands to operate them.

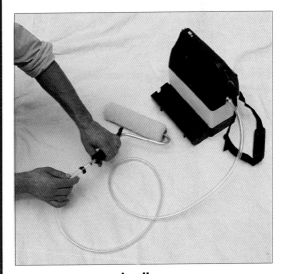

Battery-operated roller
Automatically pumps paint from an enclosed reservoir to the roller head, eliminating the need to reload the roller. Its 'back-pack' design makes it especially useful for ladder work.

Using a brush

Paintbrushes are the most versatile painting tool for a decorator's toolbox. They are manufactured in many different sizes and the qualities available vary considerably. As a general rule, the more expensive a brush is, the longer it will last and the better the painted finish will be. Pure bristle brushes are still the best option although synthetic varieties are available.

TOOLS: Paintbrushes, paint kettle

MATERIALS: Paint, lint-free cloth

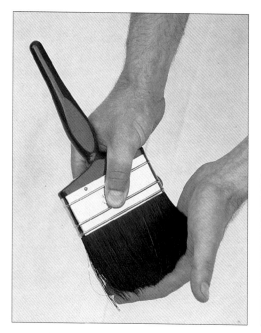

1 Before starting to paint, flick the end of the bristles and wipe them on a lint-free cloth to remove any loose bristles and dust. New brushes should be first used to prime wood or apply an undercoat, to get rid of any remaining loose bristles. They can then be used for top coats at a later date, when they will not shed any further bristles.

2 Dip the brush into the paint in the kettle so that about one-third of the bristles are immersed. Raise the brush and gently push the bristles against the side of the kettle to get rid of excess paint. Avoid scraping the bristles against the rim of the kettle as this will build up paint on the kettle's inside edge and leave drips running down the outside.

RE-USING OLD BRUSHES
Old paintbrushes that have not been stored correctly may have bristles that stick out in all directions from the main body of the brush. It is possible to trim these away with scissors to neaten the bristles and provide a brush that will give a reasonable finish. See page 91 for tips on cleaning and storing brushes.

SOLVENT-BASED PAINT

1 When applying solvent-based paint to a large area such as a flush door, begin by painting three vertical parallel strips each of which should be about 30cm (12in) long.

2 Without reloading the brush, blend the strips together with horizontal stokes, brushing out the paint to ensure even coverage. Finally, 'lay off' the painted area with light vertical strokes.

PAINTING A WALL

1 When painting a large area with water-based paint, choose a 100–150mm (4–6in) brush. Use short, alternating horizontal and vertical strokes, applying a loaded brush only to an unpainted area and working back to a painted area. On rough surfaces, a rotating motion may help to cover surfaces completely.

2 Although rollers cover open areas quickly, it is still necessary to finish off around the edges. Brushes are the best tool to use for this, and this stage of work is known as cutting in. The dividing edge between walls and woodwork may sometimes be less than precise on the exterior of a house, so care is needed.

3 In awkward recesses, use a smaller brush. Take care not to overload it when cutting in as this can lead to a thick build-up of paint around the edge you are trying to define. Do not worry if you overlap slightly on to a window or frame which is to be painted, as this helps create a better seal.

Using a sprayer

Using a paint sprayer is a fast, efficient way of painting large surface areas. There are two main types of sprayer available.

A conventional or compressed-air sprayer feeds air from a compressor up a tube into a small reservoir of paint which is normally positioned directly below the gun, forming a distinct unit in itself. The paint is then mixed with the air and sprayed on the wall by pulling the gun's trigger.

An airless spray gun is electrically operated and relies on paint being pumped, under high pressure, from a larger reservoir or hopper up a tube to the gun and then on to the wall surface. The airless gun is easier to use as the paint remains with the rest of the machinery at ground level. The use of an airless spray gun is illustrated here.

Masking around the area to be painted is absolutely essential when using a sprayer (see pages 50–51), and never spray when the weather is windy as paint 'drift' can travel a long distance.

TOOLS: Airless sprayer, goggles, respirator mask, ladder, dust sheets

MATERIALS: Paint, thinning agent (water or white spirit), masking tape, plastic dust sheet

1 Sprayers vary in the way they are used so follow the manufacturer's guidelines precisely. However, there are some guidelines common to all.
First, make sure the sprayer is turned off at the mains. Select the correct nozzle attachment and insert it into the gun. Never point the gun at anyone or place your hands in front of the nozzle. Always make sure the gun lock is on when the sprayer is not in use and never attempt to unblock a nozzle when the sprayer is on.

2 Pour paint into the paint reservoir or hopper up to the level indicated. Some airless spray guns may not have a reservoir, so a suction tube is put into a bucket to draw the paint into the pump and the spray gun. Both types of sprayer produce the same results. The paint may require thinning. Make sure that it is suitable for spraying: for example, most airless spray guns will not spray textured paint, whereas many compressed-air sprayers will.

3 Turn the sprayer on and adjust the pressure to suit paint delivery needs. Test this by spraying a test patch.

4 Wear protective goggles and a respiratory mask when using a spray gun. Hold the gun 20–30cm (8–12in) from the wall and begin at the top working down with a constant sweeping motion as shown in the diagram below. Overlap the strips of paint slightly to get even coverage. Never dwell in one area as the paint will inevitably start dripping. Apply several thin coats rather than one or two thick ones.

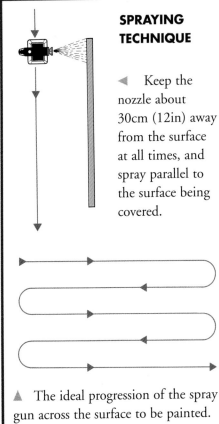

SPRAYING TECHNIQUE

◄ Keep the nozzle about 30cm (12in) away from the surface at all times, and spray parallel to the surface being covered.

▲ The ideal progression of the spray gun across the surface to be painted.

5 The versatility of a spray gun is useful when cutting in as the paint will get into the smallest, hard-to-reach areas. When the masking tape is removed a precise finish will be revealed.

6 Clean all the equipment thoroughly after use. This is normally a simple process of filling the hopper with water (or white spirit, depending on the paint used) and pumping it through the system until the spray runs clear.

Textured coatings

Coatings with an in-built texture give a hard-wearing, decorative finish and are becoming increasingly easier to apply to most prepared masonry surfaces. Although they tend to be expensive, they are durable enough to outlast any standard paint treatment.

There are two main types. Tyrolean is a coarse finish that uses a hand-held machine to splatter the coating on to the wall. Alternatively, various proprietary coatings are applied with a trowel, float, roller or even a sprayer, and then textured with a range of special tools.

TOOLS: Hawk, plastering float, 25–37mm (1–1½in) paintbrush, sponge, bucket, textured roller, texture tools

MATERIALS: Textured coating, water

SURFACES AND REQUIREMENTS

Ideally, a textured coating should be applied direct to rendered walls that have been prepared thoroughly (see pages 34–35). Most walls made from facing bricks and building blocks are also suitable, as long as their pointing is flush with the bricks or blocks.

Some manufacturers will insist that a plinth be provided at the level of the damp-proof course. Always check the manufacturer's guidelines before starting to use a textured coating, and mask up all areas before application (see pages 50–51).

COVERING CRACKS

Textured coatings are also useful for covering small cracks on a rendered surface. Larger cracks can initially be filled with the textured coating instead of filler and then a top coat applied.

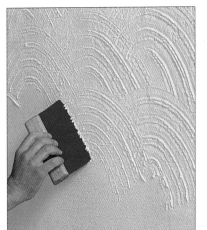

1 A textured coating may be applied with a roller or, as shown here, using a plastering float and hawk. Applying a texture is an ideal job for two people as one can float on the coating while the other follows behind, making the texture.

2 To start with, apply a layer 1–2mm (¹⁄₁₆in) thick, in areas of 1–2sq m (1–2½sq yd) at a time, taking care to smooth the surface and ensuring coverage is even. Where possible, finish coating at a natural break, as it dries quickly.

3 One way to produce a decorative finish is to run a textured roller across the surface of the coating. Then float more coating on to the next adjoining area and repeat the texturing process, keeping a wet edge going at all times.

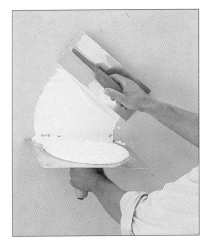

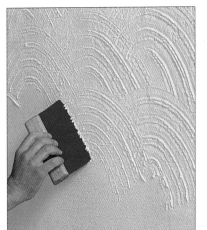

4 In awkward or small areas where the roller will not go, such as cutting in around windows or behind downpipes, dab a small paintbrush in the coating to produce the required textured effect.

5 There are many different types of texturing tool that can be used to create a variety of effects. Always practise producing a consistent pattern before you commit yourself to covering a large area.

6 Keep washing tools in clean water during application as drying paint will hinder progress. Finally, remove any masking immediately after the texturing is complete as it will be difficult after the coating has dried.

Painting a plinth

On some houses, the bottom level of the walls protrude slightly to form a plinth. This is often painted a dark colour to hide the dirt splashed up from rain drops, or just as an extra dimension to the decorative appeal of the house. It is also possible to create the effect of having a plinth by the methods outlined below.

If necessary, before starting to paint, use a spade to pull back 5–10cm (2–4in) of soil or gravel away from the base of the wall. This will help to avoid getting dirt or grit in the paintbrush and ensure a neat finish when the soil is replaced after painting is complete.

TOOLS: Hammer, 2 nails, tape measure, chalk line, spirit level, paintbrush, paint kettle

MATERIALS: Paint, 25–50mm (1–2in)-wide masking tape

1 It is important to produce a level horizontal line with a clear and precise division between the main wall colour and that of the plinth you are creating. This becomes even trickier when the ground is not level. Initially, by eye, choose a level which you feel would be a suitable height from the ground. There may be obstructions such as downpipes along the wall so it may be necessary to divide the wall into sections. Hammer in a nail at your chosen height close to the corner of the wall, or in this case, next to the natural division caused by a downpipe.

2 Attach a chalk line to the nail. If you do not have a chalk line use a piece of string and rub some ordinary household chalk along its length. Make sure the chalk colour is different from the colour of the wall.

3 Move along to the other end of the wall, holding the string close to the wall surface. Use a spirit level to make the line level. This is easier with two people as one can hold the string while the other holds the spirit level, but with a little balance and perseverance it is perfectly possible on one's own. Once certain of an exact level, hammer in another nail and tie off the string, making sure that it is tight against the wall surface.

4 Now move to the central point of the chalk line, and pull it back about 50–75mm (2–3in) from the wall. Then release the line quickly, 'snapping' it on the wall leaving a perfect, straight guideline.

5 Remove the line and nails and mask along and slightly above the chalk line left on the wall. Make sure the edge of the masking tape is firmly stuck down so that the painted line is even.

6 Paint the plinth, covering the lower edge of the masking tape but not straying over the top edge. To ensure that paint does not seep under the lower edge of the tape, start the brush strokes just on the masking tape and then brush down, away from its edge. Brush strokes in the other direction may force paint under the tape and ruin the precision of the finished line.

7 With the entire extent painted, remove the masking tape to reveal a perfect, level division. With one section of wall done you now have a starting level to continue on to the next wall, or past an obstruction, using the same technique to get a level line. On rough wall surfaces it may be impossible to mask. In such cases you may still paint a plinth by eye, using a level chalk line as a guide.

Guttering

The sole purpose of guttering is to channel water away from the house and it is therefore the exterior fitting that receives the greatest amount of attack from water. Keeping it in a sound condition protects the rest of the house and, despite its mainly functional role, painting it, or simply keeping it clean, enhances the rest of the exterior decoration.

There are two main types of guttering: plastic and metal. It can also be made of asbestos, but that is now mostly found only on older houses.

TOOLS: Bucket, sponge, trestles, filler dispenser, 25–50mm (1–2in) paintbrush, fitch

MATERIALS: Paint, gutter sealant, sugar soap, piece of card, white spirit, cloth

METAL

1 Cast-iron guttering is difficult to take down for painting, due to its weight, and because lengths tend to be bolted together and sealed at the joints. Therefore, removal could be a long process resulting in resealing every joint when replacing the gutter, so paint it in position. Painting inside the gutter will sustain its life, make water run-off more efficient and reduce the risk of loose material building up, causing blockages. Proprietary metal paints are ideal for all metal guttering except aluminium.

2 Use a fitch to reach inaccessible areas that must be painted to prevent damage. It is also ideal for cutting in around the brackets.

3 To prevent any splashes of paint getting on to a newly painted wall, when painting the back of downpipes, hold a piece of cardboard behind the pipe in order to shield the wall.

ASBESTOS

As it is considered a health risk, ideally guttering made from asbestos should be replaced. However, if you do decide to paint it, wear protective clothing, which must include a respiratory mask. Never sand asbestos as the dust caused is dangerous if breathed in. If you have to remove any flaky paint, damp the paint, then carefully remove the loose flakes with a scraper.

If you wish to paint the guttering with an oil-based gloss, prime any bare patches with an alkali-resistant primer. However, a water-based paint is better as it may be applied direct to the asbestos surface and its permeability allows the surface of the asbestos to breathe, reducing the risk of the paint blistering.

PLASTIC

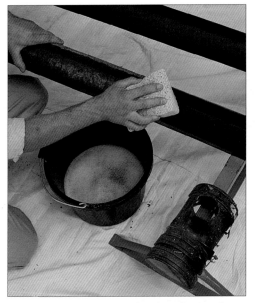

2 After many years, bleaching by the sun can discolour the guttering. Painting will return the guttering to its bright former state. No primer is required: one or two coats of gloss applied directly to the cleaned-down surface is all that is needed.

3 Once the guttering is replaced, run some water along the channel to check for any leaks. These tend to occur on a joint between two lengths and are usually the result of the

1 Plastic guttering is fast becoming the most popular type, because it is easy to maintain. It is easy to unclip and remove (see pages 24–25) in order to gain access to fascia boards. It may also be simply cleaned down using a sugar soap or mild detergent solution, making the need for painting unnecessary.

rubber seal having perished. In any problem areas, unclip the joint and dry all surfaces thoroughly. Run a bead of gutter sealant around the affected area and clip the gutter back together. Remove any excess sealant quickly with a cloth dampened in white spirit. Gutter sealant is available in a number of colours to match the existing guttering, and may be used on plastic or metal joints as a waterproofing remedy that is flexible and resistant to cracking.

Doors

Exterior doors bear the brunt of the elements, such as sun and rain, plus added wear from frequent opening and closing, making them even more liable to cracking joints, knocks and dents. In addition, the front door tends to be a focal point in the appearance of the house and so achieving the best finish possible should be a priority.

Take time to ensure you carry out the task correctly and bear in mind that, because of unavoidable wear and tear, doors may need painting more regularly than other areas.

TOOLS: Trestles, dust sheet 37mm (1½in) paintbrush, 50mm (2in) paintbrush

MATERIALS: Paint

PANELLED DOORS

1 Front doors are usually more solid than internal doors, in order to stand up to the demands asked of them. However, without care they will deteriorate quickly and are expensive to replace, so always pay particular attention to hidden areas such as underneath the weather board at the bottom. Water can seep up through this area if unprotected.

2 Before painting the rest of the door, remove it from its hinges and lay it on trestles. Work first on the bottom of the door and the weather board. Apply knotter if necessary, primer-undercoat and gloss. By using water-based paint, this operation can be completed in a day so that the door can be replaced before nightfall.

3 Drips and runs of wet paint are always a problem when painting vertical surfaces, in particular where there are protruding panels or corners where paint can collect. So, once you have finished painting the door, return to it at regular intervals during the drying time to remove any drips or runs that may have formed.

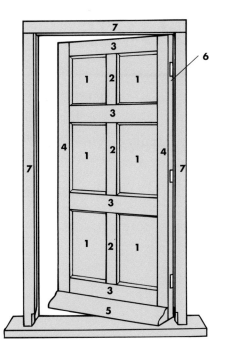

ORDER OF WORK

This diagram shows both the best sequence in which to paint a panel door and where the dividing line is between the interior and exterior.

1 Panels, working from left to right and downwards.

2 Central stiles, from the top downwards.

3 Members from top downwards.

4 Hanging stile, then locking stile.

5 Weather board.

6 Hanging edge.

7 Frame.

To get access to all the door edges, and to reduce the risk of interruption due to rain and the problem of dust and insects getting on the newly painted surface, open the door inwards before painting. Remove all accessories, such as handles and door knockers, before painting.

If possible, do not paint the hinges as the paint will crack and flake away very quickly.

FLUSH DOORS

1 Mentally divide the door into eight sections. Begin by painting in the top left-hand corner, then move to the right and downwards. A 50mm (2in) brush is ideal for this job and take care not to overload the wet edges of each section as this can easily lead to paint runs and sagging.

2 Continue to paint the door, working on one section at a time. Finish off the job by painting the door frame and the edges of the door, using a smaller brush.

PRESERVING DOOR SILLS

If wooden door sills are painted, they will be damaged quickly with chips and scuffs caused by people walking over them. It is more successful to treat them with a wood preservative or stain that can better absorb wear and tear.

Casement windows

Shapes and sizes of casement windows vary, but they are a very common type of window.

Make sure that all opening casements (lights) are partially open to allow movement, and access to edges and internal rebates. Check that these often neglected areas have been cleared of cobwebs and dust during preparation.

Paint casement windows in a logical sequence to save time on what could otherwise be a painstaking procedure. It is also best to paint them early in the day so that there is plenty of time for the paint to dry before the windows are closed in the evening.

TOOLS: 25mm (1in) paintbrush, 25mm (1in) angle-headed paintbrush, paint kettle

MATERIALS: Paint

1 Begin with the smallest opening light, painting the edges and frame rebates. Allow the light to remain slightly open to avoid sticking.

2 Paint the putty or glazing beads surrounding the window panes. A 25mm (1in) angle-headed brush makes it easier to apply the paint right into the corner of the frame. Bead the paint up to the glass edge, overlapping very slightly on to the glass to create a sealed edge. Paint the central glazing bar at the same time.

3 Finish this first opening light by painting the horizontal rails, and then the vertical rails. Take care that paint does not run down to the bottom of the light, making it hard to close later.

4 Repeat the same sequence of steps with the large opening casement or light, again making sure that it is not closed once painted, to avoid sticking.

METAL AND PVC WINDOWS

Metal windows that are normally painted are prepared and repainted in exactly the same way as their wooden counterparts. However, if there are any patches of rust, they should be cleaned back to sound, bare metal and initially treated with metal primer.

Aluminium and PVC windows are specifically designed to require very little maintenance. They should not be painted. To keep them clean and bright, wash them down during decoration with warm soapy water. Never use abrasive cleaners on either aluminium or PVC as they may scratch and disfigure the surface.

5 Paint the sealed casement. There are no edges to worry about here, so begin with the putty or beads followed by the glazing bars, and work out to the horizontal and vertical rails.

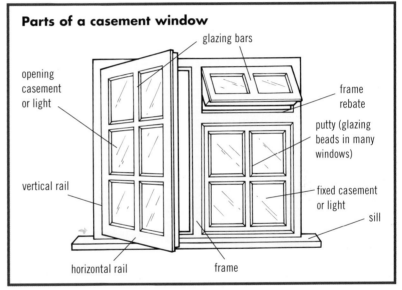

Parts of a casement window

glazing bars

opening casement or light

frame rebate

putty (glazing beads in many windows)

vertical rail

fixed casement or light

sill

horizontal rail

frame

6 Paint the frame. You may need to open the casements to do this, before returning them to a position just ajar.

7 Finish off by painting the window sill, being sure to paint the underside. Most sills have a small groove or drip guard stretching the length of the underside to prevent water running back to the wall where it may penetrate between the wood and masonry. Therefore, make sure that this groove is clear of obstruction and that there is not too much paint build up along it, which would reduce its effectiveness.

Sash windows

Due to their design, sash windows appear to be difficult to paint, but if the correct sequence of painting is followed, they are as straightforward as any other job. If the runners are sound and no colour change is required, they should not be repainted as too many coats of paint will make the window jam.

As with all windows, begin painting them at the start of the day so they are dry and ready to close at nightfall.

TOOLS: 37–50mm (1½–2in) paintbrush, fitch, paint kettle, window guard, window scraper

MATERIALS: Paint

Parts of a sash window

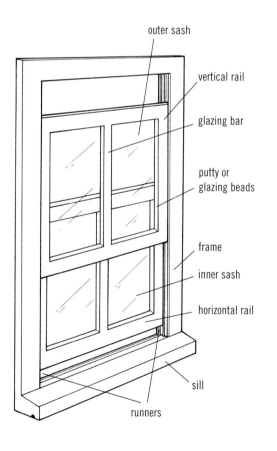

- outer sash
- vertical rail
- glazing bar
- putty or glazing beads
- frame
- inner sash
- horizontal rail
- sill
- runners

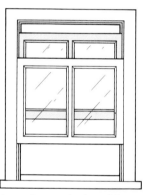

1 Lift the inner sash nearly to the top of the frame and lower the outer sash to about half way down the frame. Paint the top half of the inner sash beginning with the putty or glazing beads, followed by the glazing bar, and then the vertical and horizontal rails, including the top edge of the upper horizontal rail. If required, paint the top sections of the external runners.

2 Lower the inner sash to a slightly open position and push the outer sash nearly to the top of the window frame. Finish painting the inner sash and begin to paint the outer sash, starting with the putty or glazing beads.

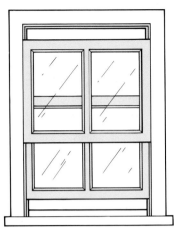

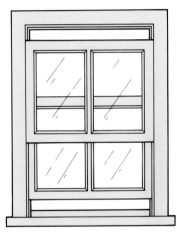

3 Complete the outer sash by painting the glazing bar, the vertical and horizontal rails, including the bottom edge of the lower horizontal rail. Paint the other half of the outer runner, if needed.

4 Finish the window by painting the window frame and finally the sill, including the underside and checking that the drip guard is clear (see step 7, page 71).

Parts of a sash window – mechanism

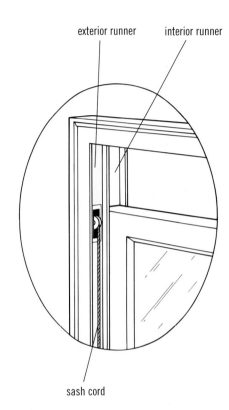

exterior runner   interior runner

sash cord

IDEAL TOOLS

Window guard

Saves time by keeping paint off the glass. Hold the guard tight up against the glass and the rebate, paint around the pane and move the guard along to the next area. Window guards are less effective on older widows, as undulating rebates and small joint variations allow paint to squeeze out under the guard's edges. Wipe it clean frequently to avoid paint build-up and smudging.

Window scraper

Handy for removing paint overspill or spray from the glass of the window once the paint has dried.

Fitch

Useful for painting the runners as it is important to keep paint clear of the sash cord, otherwise the sliding mechanism will be hampered.

Waterproofing

Although they are not at all decorative, various waterproofing substances – all of which are painted on – are vital for exterior maintenance and decoration. These include liquid rubber for felt-covered flat roofs, clear waterproofing sealant for unpainted walls and flexible sealant for the gaps that may occur around window and door frames.

In spite of their limited decorative appeal, these products provide essential protection against water penetration, and are especially useful for surfaces that are particularly vulnerable to weathering. They have a longer lifespan than other painting products, so rest assured you will not have to use them every time you redecorate.

TOOLS: Stiff brush, old 50–75mm (2–3in) paintbrush, hawk, trowel, broom, gloves, respirator mask, goggles, filler dispenser, filler knife

MATERIALS: Cement and sand mix, waterproofing sealer, liquid rubber primer, liquid rubber, masking tape, frame sealant

WATERPROOFING AND SEALING WALLS

Clear liquid waterproofers do not change the appearance of the surface to which they have been applied. Paint can generally be applied over them if required (although a time lapse of weeks rather than days may be needed for application of water-based paints).

1 Surfaces must be filled before waterproofing. Rake out any decaying mortar from between bricks and repoint using about 1 part cement to 6 parts sand mix. This mix will vary according to the exact surface; most building merchants will happily supply advice on composition.

2 The quickest and easiest way to brush down an exterior wall, to remove any loose material, is to use an ordinary household broom.

3 Most types of waterproofing sealers are supplied in metal screw-top cans with a trigger spray and attachment that is easily connected to the spout of the can. This is an efficient method for applying the sealer, but if you are using it, be sure to wear protective gloves and a respiratory mask. On very porous surfaces, two coats will be required.

FLAT ROOFS

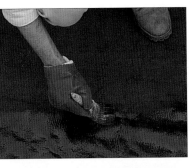

1 Remove loose and flaky material with a stiff brush. Treat with a fungicidal wash if it is mouldy and fill any large holes with an exterior mastic filler. Make sure the roof is dry before proceeding.

2 Once the roof is quite dry, use an old brush to apply one generous coat of liquid rubber primer. Allow it to dry but only until the surface becomes tacky. This tackiness makes a better bond between the primed surface and the coats of liquid rubber sealant that will be applied on top.

3 Liquid rubber is usually self levelling and can therefore be poured from the can direct on to the roof surface. However it is more than likely that small depressions in the roof mean you must move the rubber over the surface with an old brush to make sure of even coverage. Two thin coats should be applied rather than one thick one.

FRAME SEALANT

Due to its flexible, rubbery nature, frame sealant is notoriously difficult to apply and finish neatly. It can sometimes help to mask the area to be filled.

There is some colour choice with these sealants so choose carefully, either to match the paintwork or the colour of the masonry.

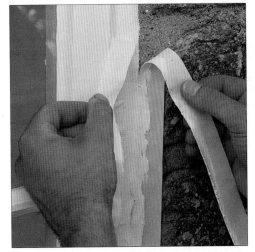

1 To ensure a neat finish, apply masking tape down either side of the crack. Run the sealant down the crack by applying a constant pressure to the trigger of the filler dispenser.

2 If necessary, smooth the bead of sealant off with a filler knife that has been wetted with a mild detergent solution. Then remove the masking tape immediately, before the sealant cures, otherwise it might be pulled off.

Metal

Apart from guttering and downpipes (see pages 66–67) there are a number of other metallic items that are often found on the exteriors of houses. Painting these smaller accessories will add considerably to the overall decorative finish, as well as prolong the life of the objects, so they should not be overlooked.

Some metal surfaces will require specific primers before a finishing paint may be applied, and so it is important to use the correct type and order of coats for a lasting finish.

TOOLS: 15–75mm (½–3in) paintbrushes, wire brush, roller cage, roller sleeve, roller tray, paint kettle, gloves

MATERIALS: Paint, aerosol paint, proprietary metal paint

CAST IRON

1 Before painting a ferrous metal such as cast iron, use a wire brush to remove any loose, flaky material.

2 Apply one, or two coats if required, of a proprietary metal finishing paint direct to the bare and previously painted metal surface. There is no need for primers with this type of finishing paint, and therefore a great deal of time is saved while still achieving an excellent decorative and protective finish.

A thinners-based solvent may be required for cleaning brushes, so be sure to check the manufacturer's guidelines before you start.

EASIER PAINTING

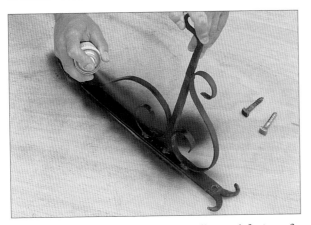

It is often easier to take down small metal fittings for painting. An intricately designed object, such as a hanging basket bracket, can be painted very quickly using aerosol paint. Spray such items on a wooden board which acts as a non-stick surface while the object is drying.

GARAGE DOORS

On large metallic surface areas, such as garage doors, proprietary metal finishing paints are not ideal. Although the preservative qualities of the paint are good, the decorative finish tends to be slightly patchy and inconsistent. It is therefore better to use an appropriate metal primer (see below left), undercoat and gloss. Most new garage doors will be supplied having been primed at the factory, so only undercoat and gloss are required.

GALVANISED METAL

Non-ferrous metal surfaces often require a specific primer before any finishing paint can be applied. For example, galvanised metal has a corrosion-resistant metal such as zinc deposited on its ferrous surface to give it added protection. Should such a surface require painting, use a proprietary metal primer designed for galvanised metals, before applying any finishing paint.

METAL MESH

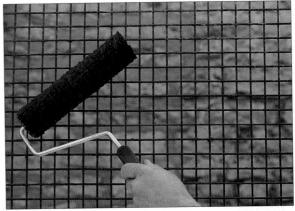

Metallic mesh fencing or trellises can sometimes require painting. At first glance this would appear impossible, or a job that would take forever with a brush. After cleaning down with a wire brush, simply apply a proprietary finishing paint using a roller. Make sure that compared to the amount of paint used for walls, the roller head is underloaded to avoid drips and runs.

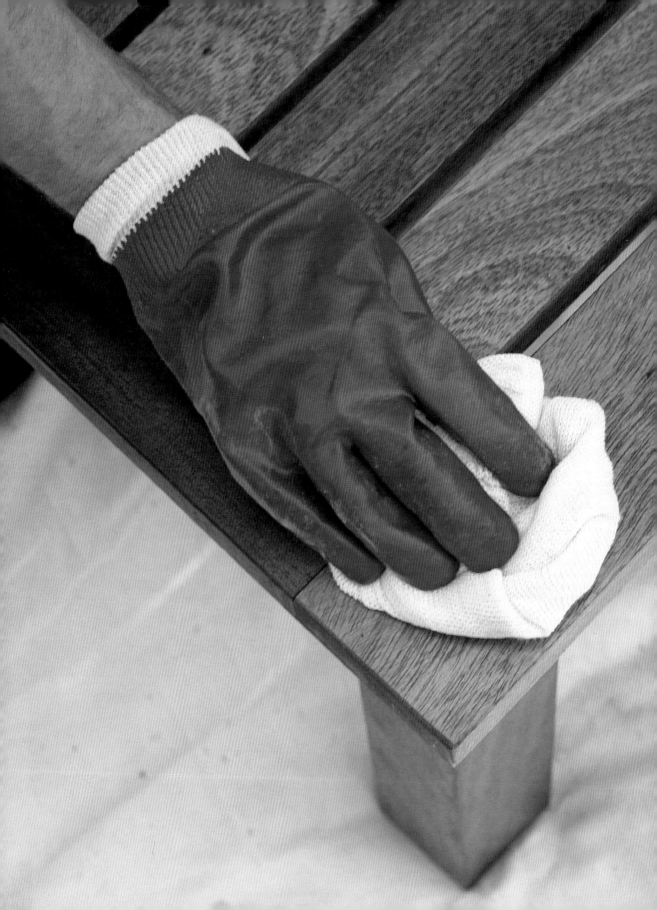

Natural Wood Finishes

There are two options for decorating and preserving wood: to paint it, or to apply a more 'natural' looking finish and allow the beautiful grain of wood to show. Stains, dyes, varnishes and oils all add a further dimension to exterior painting as well as being excellent preservatives.

Consider more than the fixed items, such as windows and doors. Garden furniture, for example, can be used to contrast with a painted house or blend attractively with other wooden features such as fences and the garden as a whole.

Preparation

If you wish to apply a natural wood finish to a presently painted surface or to most stained or varnished surfaces whose colour you wish to change, it is necessary to strip off all existing coatings (see pages 38–39). However, it is possible to avoid complete stripping if you are applying a 'maintenance' stain or varnish coat to a previously treated surface of the same colour.

It is important to remember when buying preparatory materials for natural wood finishes that the translucent qualities of stains or varnishes have specific requirements. For example, they will not disguise filler unless it is specifically designed to match the wood or finish colour.

TOOLS: Scraper, sanding block, dusting brush, fitch, putty knife, hot-air gun

MATERIALS: Stainable filler, sandpaper, lint-free cloth, white spirit, protective base coat, stain/varnish, wood reviver, coloured putty

MAINTENANCE COAT

1 First remove any loose, flaky material with a scraper, and fill any cracks or holes with a stainable filler.

2 Working along the grain of the wood, sand back both the filled areas and the remainder until a smooth surface is achieved.

3 Dust off all surfaces and wipe them down with a lint-free cloth dampened with a little white spirit.

REPAIRING PUTTYWORK

When repairing putty, use a colour that closely matches the existing one, as standard white putty will not stain effectively to provide a match. Ideally, replace all the putty with glazing beads as they will last longer. As well, they are essential if varnish is chosen as, generally, putty will not accept varnish.

TREATING KNOTS

Bleeding or seeping knots will often spoil a natural wood finish. To render them inactive, use a hot-air gun to draw the sap out of the wood, scraping away the residue until no more appears. Take care not to scorch the wood surface with the hot-air gun as it will spoil the eventual finish.

4 'Touch in' the bare areas of wood with a protective base coat if required (see pages 14–15). Allow it to dry and then touch in with the same coloured stain or varnish that was used on the previous decoration.

The old, sound coating will now be matched in with the newly coated bare areas and the surface will be ready for the required number of top coats (see pages 14–15).

REVIVING OLD WOOD

Where surface coatings have almost completely weathered away or the wood has become denatured and lacks colour, it is possible to breathe some life back into it before decoration. First, any areas of rot should be treated and filled in exactly the same manner as for painted surfaces (see pages 40–43) except the wood filler used must be stainable and able to receive a natural wood finish. Sand back the surface of the wood to remove any powdery or decaying material, and thoroughly rub in a coat of wood reviver.

Wood stains

These versatile and decorative wood treatments come in a large range of colours, from those that accentuate the wood's natural colour to those that can totally change the basic colour to one that you prefer. They are also produced in varying degrees of opacity, which adds to the variety of finishes available.

Although the effect of stains is usually stunning, a certain amount of care is needed during application to achieve the right result.

TOOLS: Trestles, 37–50mm (1½–2in) varnish brush, paint kettle

MATERIALS: Stain, sandpaper, white spirit, lint-free cloth

1 Most items have to be stained in position, but doors are ideal to remove from their hinges and stain flat on trestles. This avoids drips or runs and makes application far easier. Apply a base coat to the wood before staining, if recommended in the manufacturer's instructions.

2 Doors should be stained in the same order as for painting (see pages 68–69). Always stain in the direction of the grain, brushing the stain well into the surface. Take care not to overload the brush as this can result in a patchy finish with uneven coverage.

3 Try to be precise when staining the separate horizontal and vertical sections of a door, and the panels, as overlapping edges of stain and the direction of brush strokes will show through overlapping coats if not thoroughly brushed out in the direction of the grain.

4 Define each section with straight lines, never allowing a ragged edge to dry or protrude on to another surface. This would lose the clear definition of each panel, member or stile.

5 Use the brush to 'pick up' any drips along the edges. Take care not to overload the brush making the stain thicker and darker along the corners of the door.

6 Stain tends to 'lift' the surface of the wood which makes it slightly rough to the touch. Lightly sand the surface with a fine-grade sandpaper between coats, but not after the final coat. After each sanding, remove the dust and fine debris by wiping them down with a lint-free cloth dampened with a little white spirit.

7 The other advantage of taking the door off its hinges is so that the underneath of the weather board and the bottom edge of the door can be stained as well. This protects them from the inevitable penetration of rainwater, the results of which could otherwise be very damaging in the long term (see pages 68–69).

Varnishes and oils

Although stains are becoming by far the most popular form of natural wood finish, varnishes and oils are an alternative choice with their own particular qualities.

Varnish is a translucent sealing coat. Traditional forms are high-gloss, but various mid-sheen finishes are also available, with colour choice growing all the time. Varnish can be applied over most previously stained surfaces and as a maintenance coat when appropriate (see pages 80–83). The main drawback of varnish is that it will not last as long as stain and therefore requires recoating more frequently.

Oil is a more penetrative, wood-nourishing application which is ideally suited to hardwoods such as teak.

TOOLS: Gloves, 37–50mm (1½–2in) varnish brush, paint kettle

MATERIALS: Varnish, oil, lint-free cloth, old tin

1 When varnishing bare wood it may be necessary to apply a protective base coat before the varnish itself. This is common when using solvent-based varnishes. When using some base coats, wear protective gloves.

2 If using a base coat, allow it to dry for the time specified by the manufacturer. Then apply the first coat of varnish, initially with vertical up-and-down strokes at right angles to the grain of the wood.

3 Before the vertical strokes begin to dry, immediately lay off the varnish with horizontal strokes in the direction of the grain. This method of vertical and horizontal brushing helps ensure total coverage.

WOOD OILS

The colour range of wood oils is limited as the wood colour itself is relied upon to provide the decorative aspect of the treatment. Oil should be reapplied every one to two years to keep the wood in a highly decorative condition but doing this is not too arduous as it is very quick to apply. The preservative qualities of oil will last longer than this period, so if a more weathered, natural look is required, such regular coatings are not completely necessary.

1 Apply the oil liberally along the direction of the grain, making sure it saturates the wood completely. When oiling outdoor furniture, as shown here, turn it over in order to soak the base of each leg to prevent water penetration.

2 Before the oil dries, remove any excess from the surface of the wood, by buffing it with a lint-free cloth. This will slightly polish the wood surface, giving the finish a light sheen.

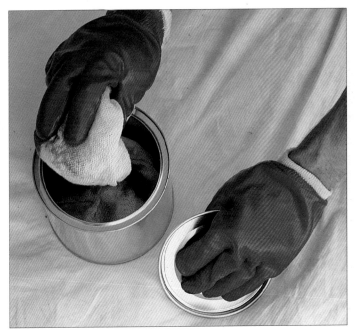

3 Oily rags are highly flammable and can even spontaneously combust. Soiled rags should therefore be placed in a water-filled metal container, sealed and disposed of safely. This method is also acceptable for temporary storage, but keep the container outside only.

Preservatives

Applying timber preservative is one of the quicker exterior painting jobs because preparation is minimal. Either the wood is rough, or a finely sanded, highly polished finish is not necessary. Most preservatives are applied to large surface areas, so speed up the process by using large brushes.

Because timber preservatives are quite thin, there is a tendency for them to drip, run and fly everywhere during application. Overalls are therefore essential and goggles and gloves should be worn, depending on the manufacturer's recommendations. As well, be sure to put dust sheets over grass and flower beds as these chemicals may damage plants.

TOOLS: Overalls, stiff brush, dust sheet, goggles, gloves, 75–100mm (3–4in) paintbrush, airless spray gun, bucket, paint kettle, respirator mask

MATERIALS: Timber preservative

FENCES

1 Before coating a wooden fence with a timber preservative the only major preparation required is to remove any cobwebs, lichen growth and loose material, such as dead plant matter, from the surface using a stiff brush.

2 Apply the preservative liberally, in order to totally saturate the wood. Because the liquid penetrates deeply into the wood, most runs and drips will soak in, so painting and brush technique is not crucial when working on such a surface.

3 If you have to replace an old fence post or are erecting a new fence, soak the bottom of the post(s) in a bucket of preservative overnight. A post will be open to attack below ground level so this ensures protection when the base is buried.

TRELLISES

A trellis can seem to take forever to treat if using a brush to apply the liquid. The ideal tool is an easy-to-use, hand-held airless spray gun which covers the area in a fraction of the time. Any wastage will be more than made up for by the time saved using this technique.

Ideally, remove the trellis from its fixed position and be sure to put a dust sheet behind it to protect the backing surface against overspray.

It is essential to wear protective equipment such as a mask, gloves and goggles.

Refer to pages 60–61 for further tips on using spraying equipment.

GARDEN FURNITURE

1 Make sure the product you have chosen is safe for use on furniture, bearing in mind that such surfaces may come into contact with food that is eaten outdoors, and that children will come into contact with them.

2 Pay particular attention to the end grain of the wood, as this is where damp attack will be most likely to occur. On bare wood, two to three coats of preservative should be adequate, with maintenance coats applied every one to two years.

Problems and solutions

After decoration is complete, you may find that the finish is not quite up to the standard you had expected. There may be various faults which are instantly noticeable or which develop over the first few weeks or months after painting.

Most paint faults tend to be very localised and these can be remedied fairly simply. More extensive problems normally result from using the wrong materials or from poor preparation.

The most common complaints are outlined below, combined with a guide on how to solve them.

GRIT OR INSECTS IN PAINT

Even slight breaths of wind will blow grit or dirt on to wet painted surfaces. A perfect finish is therefore difficult to achieve outside, so a compromise needs to be sought between what is acceptable and what needs further attention. On particularly 'gritted' surfaces, sand back and repaint. Insects offer a similar problem as they always seem to find their way on to wet paint. Leave the paint to dry thoroughly and then use a dry cloth or dusting brush to clear them from the surface. You will be surprised how easily they clear, with little damage to the paint.

POOR COVERAGE ON MASONRY

Wall surface simply requires another coat of paint. Often occurs when trying to cover a dark colour with light or if paint has been poorly applied on a rough surface.

POOR PAINT COVERAGE ON WOOD

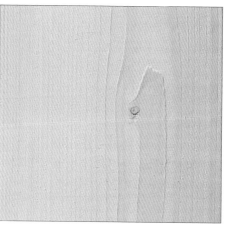

Either caused by too few coats of paint or, more seriously, not having used a primer coat on the bare wood. Strip back to bare wood and prime before repainting correctly.

LIFTING PAINT ON PUTTY

Caused by painting the putty before it has completely dried out. Remove flaking paint, allow the putty to dry thoroughly and repaint (see pages 44–45).

DRIPS/RUNS

Occur when too much paint has been used on a vertical surface. Allow the paint to dry completely, sand back until level and repaint.

RAIN AFFECTED

Even a small shower can devastate paint that is drying. Sand back and recoat in localised areas, but in severe cases stripping back to the bare surface may be necessary.

BLISTERING/BUBBLING

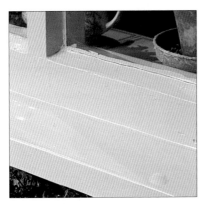

Occurs when moisture or air is trapped beneath the paint, (normally on wooden surfaces) and has expanded due to the heat caused by direct sunlight. Strip back, fill any holes if necessary and repaint. Bubbling may also be caused by painting directly on top of poorly prepared or dusty surfaces. Sand back, prepare correctly and repaint.

BRUSH MARKS IN STAIN

Can be caused by poor application. Strip back to bare wood and restain using the correct method (see pages 82–83). A similar problem occurs if stain is applied on top of a varnished surface, as the stain is unable to soak into the wood and therefore simply 'sits' on top of the varnish. Strip back to bare wood and restain.

ORANGE PEEL/WRINKLING

Caused when a solvent-based paint has been applied over a first coat which has not dried completely. Strip back to the bare surface and repaint, allowing adequate drying time between coats. Wrinkling is also commonly found on painted putty surfaces which have not had the required drying time before being painted over.

Cleaning up and storage

Once the job is complete, all equipment should be cleaned thoroughly before being put away. Do not make the common mistake of leaving brushes in a jar of white spirit and expecting them to be as good as new in six months' time, as they will simply dry out and be ruined. There are obvious savings to be made by looking after expensive brushes and rollers. Although the process may seem arduous at the time, you will be grateful when you come to tackle the next decorating project.

Remember to dispose of any empty cans or chemical debris safely.

TOOLS: Cleaning system box, scraper, brush comb, gloves

MATERIALS: Household detergent, wire wool, white spirit, glass jar, clean cloth, brown paper, rubber band, hand cleanser, proprietary masonry cleaner

WATER-BASED PAINT

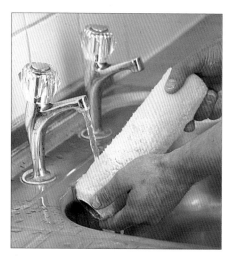

1 Clean roller sleeves by first wiping off the excess on an old board or some newspaper. Then wash the sleeve under running water until the water runs clear. This is aided by the use of a mild household detergent. Rinse and shake dry. If the roller head has been used to paint a rough surface, the amount of wear and tear it has received will often render it useless for the next painting job. In such cases, throw the roller sleeve out.

2 Wash out brushes using the same technique for rollers. To remove any dried paint, a blunt scraper can be drawn across the bristles or a brush comb used to loosen the paint. Wire wool is useful to remove paint from the ferrule of a brush, or from a metal roller cage which often becomes caked in paint.

SOLVENT-BASED PAINT

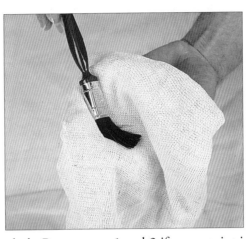

2 Take the brush out, removing the excess cleaning agent by drawing the bristles across the edge of the jar. Dry the brush thoroughly with a clean

1 Remove any excess paint from the brush and stir it vigorously in a jar of white spirit or proprietary brush cleaner.

cloth. Repeat steps 1 and 2 if excess paint is still evident in the bristles. Finally, wash the brush with warm water and detergent, rinse and shake dry.

CLEANING SYSTEM BOX

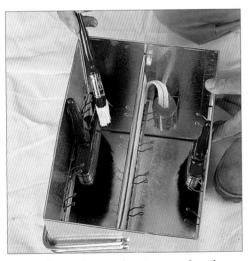

As an alternative to cleaning out brushes which have been used with solvent-based products, a proprietary cleaning system box may be used. Brushes can be stored indefinitely by suspending the drying process. Chemical vapour contained in such an enclosed space allows the bristles to remain moist and ready for use.

CLEANING UP PAINT SPOTS

Once the job is complete and all accessories have been put back in their appropriate position, it is not uncommon to find that the odd paint splash or run has found its way on to unpainted masonry or ground surfaces. Proprietary masonry cleaners are available to solve this problem. Simply spray or dab on some of the cleaning agent and wipe away with a cloth. Wear protective gloves when carrying out this task.

STORAGE

All brushes should be dry before they are put away. In order to keep them in prime condition, wrap the bristles in brown paper held in place with a rubber band. This will help the brush to keep its shape rather than allowing the bristles to splay out in all directions.

Glossary

Barge boards
Boards attached to the rafters on the exterior of a house, at the gable end.

Batten
A length of straight wood, used as a guideline.

Beading
Using the extreme edge of a paintbrush to achieve a precise dividing line between two colours or surfaces.

Blown
Where the top layer of masonry, has separated from the main block structure of the wall: eg cement render separating from a brick wall.

Casement window
A window made up of hinged and/or fixed lights.

Chalk line
A length of string covered in chalk dust, pulled tight and 'snapped' against a surface to leave a straight guideline.

Cutting in
Applying paint into an angle such as between a wall and the soffit, or on a narrow surface such as a glazing bar.

Damp-proof course
A layer of impenetrable material placed at about 150mm (6in) above ground level to prevent moisture penetration.

Dowel
A short round length of wood (ideal for stirring paint).

Fascia
Lengths of board found just below the edge of the roof, used for attaching guttering.

Feathering
Blending in uneven edges during sanding.

Flush
Term used to describe two level, adjacent surfaces.

Fungicide
A chemical that kills mould or algae.

Glazing beads
Small lengths of wood used to seal around and retain panes of glass. An alternative to putty.

Glazing pins
Small nails used to secure the position of a pane of glass or to attach glazing beads.

Hardwoods
Normally found as smooth, planed wood. Very durable and more expensive than softwoods. Most often used for exterior purposes, such as a front door. Common hardwoods include oak, teak and iroko.

Hawk
Square metal or wooden board with a vertical handle beneath. Used as a platform for holding plaster, cement, filler, or textured coatings.

Hopper
Paint reservoir on airless spray equipment.

Key
A slightly rough surface that has been sanded to provide a bond for paint.

Laying off
Light brush strokes, made in a similar direction, to eliminate brush marks left on a painted surface.

Lint-free cloth
A cloth, usually made of cotton, which does not moult fibres.

Members
Horizontal wooden struts that are part of a panelled door.

Metal finishing paint
A rust-inhibiting paint that requires no primer or undercoat.

Microporous
The property of a paint or stain that allows moisture out but not into the surface of wood.

Primer
Thinned, specially formulated paint that seals and stabilises a surface before undercoat is used.

Proud
Protruding slightly from the surrounding surface.

PVA
A multi-purpose adhesive and additive, primarily used in decorating as a sealer and bonding agent.

Rails
Horizontal and vertical struts making up all windows.

Rebate
The part of a rail that is at right angles to the pane of glass.

Render
A semi-smooth coat of sand and cement applied over a rough wall to give it a more even, protective coating.

Sash window
A window in which the opening sections – the sashes – slide up and down vertically within a frame, counterbalanced by weights held on sash cords.

Soffit
Board positioned at right angles to and below the fascia boards, to enclose the roof space.

Softwood
Normally supplied as either smooth or rough sawn. Cheaper and less durable than hardwoods. Used for all sorts of joinery, interior or exterior, such as windows or fascia boards. Common softwoods include white deal and spruce.

Stiles
Vertical struts that are part of a panelled door.

Index

The authors would like to thank the
following for their assistance in producing this book:

Access International Ltd, Maldon, Essex
Crosby Sarek Ltd, Swindon, Wiltshire
Crown Brolac Decorator Centre, Yeovil, Somerset
Dave Marsh Hardware, Castle Cary, Somerset
McDougall Rose Decorating Merchants, Altrincham, Cheshire
Sparkford Sawmills, Sparkford, Somerset
Wagner Spraytec U.K. Ltd, Banbury, Oxon
Mr and Mrs R A Crossman
Mr and Mrs R J Crossman
Mr and Mrs M G Read

Editor: Margot Richardson
Designers: Hilary Prosser and John Round

Managing Editor: Miranda Spicer
Art Director: Martin Lovelock

Photography: George Wright, Polly Wreford,
James Merrell and Tim Ridley

'Ideas and Choices' Stylist: Julian Cassell and Peter Parham
Illustrator: David Eaton

Production Manager: Kevin Perrett
Set Builder: Nigel Tate

Julian Cassell and Peter Parham have asserted their
right to be identified as the authors of this work.

First published 1996

Text, photographs and illustrations
© Haynes Publishing 1996

Published by: Haynes Publishing
Sparkford, Nr Yeovil, Somerset BA22 7JJ

British Library Cataloguing-in-Publication Data:
A catalogue record for this book is available from
the British Library.

ISBN 1 85960 111 1

Printed in France by
Imprimerie Pollina, 85400 Luçon - n° 68975 - E